D1491808

Bookbinding

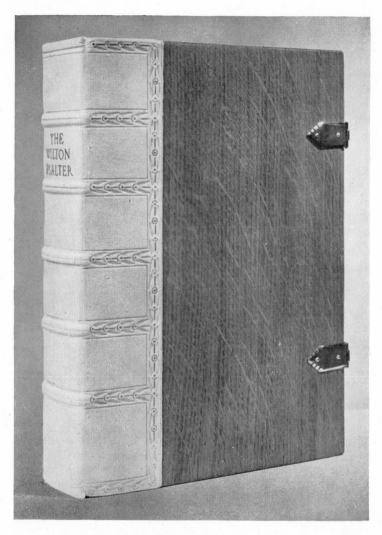

A fine modern binding for a valuable manuscript. The thirteenth-century Wilton Psalter MS bound by S. M. Cockerell in English oak boards with silver clasps and white alumed morocco spine with gold and blind tooling. Size 12 in. by 8½ in. *By kind permission of the Royal College of Physicians.*

BOOKBINDING

J. S. Hewitt-Bates, F.S.A.M.

THE DRYAD PRESS
LEICESTER

Sixth Edition 1954

Published by the Dryad Press

Printed in Great Britain at The Curwen Press Ltd., Plaistow, E.13

CONTENTS

LIST OF PLATES

NOTE ON THE AUTHOR

J. S. Hewitt-Bates, F.S.A.M., took First-Class Honours and was a First Prizeman and Silver Medallist of the City and Guilds of London Institute. As Teacher of Bookbinding, he exercised a strong influence for many years at Leicester College of Art: as a practising binder, he specialized in fine bindings and the restoration of old books. The sound principles which underlie both teaching and craftsmanship are exemplified in this latest edition of his book on the technique of binding.

FOREWORD

This book, written by one who is both a master craftsman and an experienced teacher, gives in an orderly sequence what it is necessary to know of the processes of the craft of Bookbinding. The growing interest in handwork, and the widening appreciation of its educational values, make a need for such books as this. The value of good standards of workmanship, suitable materials and appropriate finish, are rightly stressed. Being a craftsman, the author does not overlook the value of the incentive which comes from the appreciation of good work well done in a workmanlike way. So, while it is assumed that work to be done will be considered in relation to the pupil's capacity, the first exercises are in line with what may some day be finished artistry, and are directed, whatever the pupil's attainment, to the enjoyment of fine work wherever it may be.

For Bookbinding may range from simple to difficult things: from very elementary exercises suitable for children, to the skilled artistic work of the master craftsman. And exercises in binding may be co-ordinated with other school work and be put to everyday uses in many pleasant ways. The craft offers opportunities for technical as well as artistic experiment, and is one which can be developed as an after-school interest or occupation. It is well to remember in this connection that three of the most notable contributors to the craft in recent times have been amateurs: William Morris, who revived the use of beautiful pigskin bindings in such noble books as the Kelmscott Chaucer, and developed the use of flexible vellum bindings for smaller books; T. J. Cobden-Sanderson, who may be said to have established a fine English tradition based on impeccable workmanship and beautiful detail; and Sir Edward Sullivan, whose 'Cottage' designs are the most notable Irish bindings produced in the nineteenth century. These men pursued the craft for the love of it, and, with little more than the simplest equipment, produced work which is good enough to enrich our National museums and is a reminder of the many ways still open for fruitful experiment.

In few crafts are the value of careful planning, foresight, reasoned sequence of processes and good workmanship more evident, or more repaying in the result. And, contrariwise, unsuitable and badly chosen materials, careless handling, and bad finish too often bring the craft to shame. For good workmanship implies a form of integrity which avoids shoddy, slipshod work, shams and imitations: chooses good paper instead of imitation cloth, good cloth instead of imitation vellum. Good workmanship is transparently honest and, as is shown in early bindings, wins beauty—the grace of good craftsmanship—from pleasing emphasis of construction and right making. These things are not to be covered up, hidden. In the long run poor forwarding proclaims itself through showy finishing. However carefully a good tradition is followed, there will always be opportunity for personal judgement and taste in the choice among possible alternatives and in adjustment of means to new needs and conditions.

If you would learn a craft, says Samuel Butler, go into the workshop of one who earns his living by it. This book offers such an opportunity.

B. J. FLETCHER

AUTHOR'S PREFACE

Bookbinding is a craft too often neglected in school and college, though its study demands valuable artistic and practical training.

Having this consideration in mind, the aim of this book is to assist the teacher of Art and Crafts in primary and secondary schools and training colleges, by presenting the subject from a simple and practical angle that will give due regard to the educational value of the processes described.

After chapters on general matters, the teacher is provided with a series of exercises in binding, progressing in difficulty, and each logically based on the knowledge previously gained. At the same time, the subject is treated from the point of view of the experienced craftsman with regard to soundness in practical work.

It will thus be shown that experiment, art and craftsmanship, combine to make this fascinating craft a subject to be most profitably included in the school handwork scheme.

Written at the request of many of my pupils and colleagues, the book has been materially helped by their suggestions, and in the illustrations every drawing and diagram has been designed to speak for itself.

My best thanks are due to Mr. B. J. Fletcher, late Director of Art Education, Birmingham, for the Foreword and for much kindly help and inspiration during my thirty-five years' teaching.

CHAPTER I

A SHORT HISTORY OF BOOKBINDING

The History of Bookbinding is essentially linked with that of writing; as the nature of the materials and forms used determined the method of preservation. Possibly the earliest writing was that scratched or chiselled on rocks and stone pillars or tablets. Later clay was used for the purpose; stamps were made by which it was impressed, and then submitted to the action of the sun or fire to harden, then tablets of slate, lead, wood, bone, skins of animals, ivory, and even plates of gold were used. Palm leaves were perhaps the earliest pliable material used for writing purposes. Evidence is not wanting that many of these writings have been preserved, as many specimens are in our museums today.

The word 'book' is probably derived from the same root as 'beech', Anglo-Saxon 'boc', German 'buch', Dutch 'beuke', the bark of this tree having been anciently used for writing in most of the northern countries of Europe.

The Greek names 'byblos' or 'biblion' are derived from the Egyptian papyrus, and the Latin word 'liber' from the same source.

An event of the greatest importance in the history of writing and bookbinding was the invention of papyrus by the Egyptians about 4000 B.C. Great skill was displayed in the preparation of this material for writing purposes. It was made from the stem of the papyrus plant, a kind of reed that grew in the marshes in Egypt. The outer concentric layers of the stalk were first separated into thin sheets by means of a needle; two or more sheets were then laid on one another crosswise, covered with a thin paste, and rolled or beaten to weld the fibres together, and dried in the sun. The sheets thus obtained were afterwards coated over with a

B

preparation that gave them an even surface and made them pliant and flexible.

By joining the sheets thus formed, rolls of any length could be obtained, and frequently twenty or more were employed for a single manuscript.

Pens of reed were used for writing. Such pens are still in common use throughout the East. The ink was made from lamp-black, burnt ivory, charcoal, sepia, etc.; the particles being ground very fine and suspended in gum water.

At first the writing was in short lines across the rolls; at each end a roller would be attached, and the reader would unroll and roll as he read. Sometimes the writing was in long lines the length of the roll; later in columns across the roll. There is no doubt that the writing in columns suggested folding as being more convenient to read and for storage. This form led to the sewing of the back folds together, as is still done in China and Japan. The first step in bookbinding was thus evolved. The oldest manuscript known written in this form is the 'Papyrus Prisse', in the Louvre at Paris, consisting of eighteen pages in Egyptian hieratic writing, ascribed to about 2500 B.C. The rolls were often put for further protection into cylindrical cases, called 'Capsa' or 'Scrinium', frequently made of beech wood, and stored in 'The House of Rolls'. The Romans called the roll 'volumen', hence our word—volume.

A still nearer approach to modern binding was made by the Romans in their 'pugillaria', or table books. They consisted of from two to eight leaves made of ivory, wood or metal, with raised edges, and covered with wax to take the impression of the stylus. They were connected at the back by rings or thongs of leather. These pugillaria, much more than the rolls, suggested a cover, which at first was of sheep or other skin; afterwards boards were attached.

With the introduction of parchment both writing and bookbinding were much advanced. Successive experiments in the manufacture of skins for writing purposes led to the invention of vellum and parchment. This discovery is attributed to the prohibition of the exportation of papyrus from Egypt, by one of the Ptolemys, in order to throw an obstacle in the way of Eumenes,

King of Pergamus, who endeavoured to rival him in the magnificence of his library. Thus, left without material for writing on, we find that Eumenes invented a method of cleaning skins on both sides; before they could only be written on one.

The word 'parchment' is said to be derived from Pergamentum, a city in Asia Minor, where the sheep skins were first prepared about the year 190 B.C. Vellum treated in the same way as parchment is made from calf skin.

At first the parchment was written on as were the papyrus rolls, but later Eumenes adopted the method of writing on separate leaves on both sides; hence the folded form came into use. The sheets were folded once, and gatherings of four or more folded sheets were made, so that stitches through the fold at the back would hold all the sheets together, and each leaf could be conveniently turned over.

Very soon the obvious plan of fixing several of these gatherings, or sections, together by fastening the threads at the back round a strong strip of leather or vellum was adopted. This early plan of 'sewing' is today used in the case of best bound books; it is known as 'flexible' sewing, and has never been improved upon.

When the method of sewing sections together in this way became known, it was found that the projecting bands at the back needed protection, so that when the book was sewn, strips of leather were fastened all over the back. It was also found that the parchment leaves were apt to curl, and to counteract this tendency wooden boards were put on each side, the loose ends of the bands were laced into the boards and the protecting strip of leather at the back was drawn over the boards far enough to cover the lacing-in of the bands. So we get what is now termed 'quarterbinding'.

The tendency of wood to warp and crack led to the use of sheets of papyrus or parchment pasted together and heavily pressed—this formed a strong and tough material, which when dry would not crack, shrink or warp.

To the East we must look for the most marked advance in the art of bookbinding

Recent research and discoveries have proved that the Copts, an intelligent and cultured Christian race, direct descendants of the Ancient Egyptians, were well advanced in the art of writing and bookbinding in the second century of our era. The newly discovered Bible texts of papyri from Egypt assigned to the second century are all written in Codex form—i.e. in sections like modern books. This form was used by the Christians at a time when pagans still adhered to the roll.

Later we come to the massive books which were carried in the public processions of the Byzantine Emperors in the fifth century; doubtless these mighty records of the nation's laws and sacred manuscripts impressed the populace with awe and added to the dignity of the sovereign ruler. The bindings of these splendid volumes were in red, blue or yellow leather, and thin golden rods were placed across the back.

In the sixth century these 'Byzantine Coatings', as they were called, were decorated by the silversmith—the binder was only allowed to sew the leaves together and fasten them into the wooden boards. In this state they were passed on to the silversmith, who covered them with beaten gold and silver, into which jewels and precious stones were introduced

A century or two later we find that the monks were almost the only 'literati'. They wrote chiefly upon subjects of religion, and bestowed great pains upon the internal and external decoration of their books. They not only transcribed and bound books, but they prepared the parchment for their manuscripts, and the leather for the binding.

An interesting example of monastic writing and binding in the seventh century is that of a book, usually known as St. Cuthbert's Gospel. It is one of the earliest known examples of the semi-uncial style of writing in Britain and, if the binding is contemporary, the earliest known decorated leather binding in Europe. It was found in St. Cuthbert's coffin in 1105 and is now in the library of Stonyhurst College.

'It was written by Eadfrid, bishop of Durham, and Ethelwold, his successor, executed the illuminations and capitals, with infinite labour and elegance, Bilfred, a monk of Durham, is said to have covered the book and adorned it with gold and silver plates set with precious stones.' These particulars are related by Aldred, the Saxon glossator, on the fly-leaves at the end of St. John's Gospel. The vellum fly-leaves of the book, however, were added at a much later date, and have caused some doubts as to the early date of the present binding.

Many curious tales are related concerning this book: amongst others, Turgot gravely asserts that when the monks of Lindisfarne were removing from thence, to avoid the depredations of the Danes, the vessel wherein they were embarked oversetting, this book which they were transporting with them fell into the sea. Through the merits of St. Cuthbert, the sea ebbing much further than usual, it was found upon the sands, about three miles from the shore, without having received any injury from the water.

The present binding of this volume is in red leather, either russia or goat skin. In the centre of the front cover is a repoussé Celtic design; above and below are small oblong panels filled with inter-laced work executed with a style, and coloured with yellow paint. As to the date of this binding there are different opinions, some assigning it to as early as the seventh century, others the twelfth.

Mr. Douglas Cockerell, an authority on ancient bindings, writes of this volume: 'The early date is not universally admitted, mainly because it is difficult to believe that a binding could have survived the known vicissitudes of St. Cuthbert's coffin without damage.

'However, as the manuscript itself shows no serious signs of damage, we may, I think, suppose that the conditions that have led to the preservation of the manuscript have preserved the bind-ing. The little book probably had a stout leather outer case, and it may well have been preserved and carefully cherished as a holy relic apart from the coffin, and only have been placed in the outer coffin for convenience of transport.

'The ornament is such as we might expect to be produced under the Lindisfarne tradition, and nothing we know of at all like it was produced in the twelfth century, when it has been suggested the book might have been rebound.'

A detailed history of this book is given, as it shows that all the essential features of good binding were practised in England at that early date.

In the eight and ninth centuries bookbinding as an elaborate art is said to have made great progress in the age of Charlemagne, when Italian artists and craftsmen were employed. It is unfortunate that none of these bindings have been preserved, as an examination of them might have assisted us in forming a more accurate idea of the progress of the art in this period.

Then the art was neglected for several centuries, owing to the plunder and pillage that overran Europe, and books were destroyed to secure the jewels and metals with which they were covered.

In the twelfth century it is claimed that England was still ahead of all European nations as regards binding. Winchester, London, Durham and other monasteries had each their school of binding. Their books were covered with stag-hide, calf, and pig skin, and were tooled with numbers of small engraved blocks in the Gothic style.

This method of forcibly impressing from metal stamps in blind-tooling had a sobering effect on the bookbinder's art—the elaborate work of the silversmith gradually gave way to this more legitimate means of decoration by the actual binder himself.

The method of making blind impressions from engraved metal dies is claimed by Mr. Weale to be of English origin, and may have led to the invention of printing. In the light of modern research, however, it has been discovered that the Copts were familiar with 'blind-tooling', either by heated tools or with metal punches, before the sixth century.

Although the majority of medieval leather bindings are decorated with engraved metal stamps, contemporary with these there were produced a number of remarkable bindings, the decoration of which was worked with a blunt, pointed tool or cut into the surface of the leather. (This method was much the same as now used on our modern embossed leatherwork.) Generally the design is impressed on the surface of the leather and the background stippled, making the pattern stand out in apparent relief.

The majority of such bindings are of German and Austrian origin, but there are also specimens from Italy and England in the British Museum.

In the Middle Ages many bindings were brought from the East by the Crusaders, which no doubt helped to mould the destinies of bookbinding.

Towards 1465 the Saracenic patterns on Venetian books began to be sprinkled with gold dots. This innovation gradually sealed the fate of blind-tooling.

The invention of printing by Gutenberg in 1438 entirely changed the character of bookbinding. As a rule wooden boards clasps, and gold ornaments were laid aside and leather and parchments became of ordinary use. The printer at first was his own binder, but as books increased in number, bookbinding became a separate trade, and as a consequence of men applying themselves to one craft, the art improved so much that in the fifteenth and sixteenth centuries some of the finest specimens of bookbinding were executed.

About the year 1470 gold tooling by means of engraved stamps (as used at the present time) was introduced into Venice, and under the patronage of Maioli and Grolier a new and beautiful method of decorating books came into fashion. Their designs were, of course, influenced by the then dominant style of decoration, namely the Renaissance: while Byzantine in its original elements, it also has a mixture of Venetian and Norman ornament. It reasserted the aesthetic principle, and attained its highest pitch of excellence in the sixteenth century. It is little wonder that this style gained such favour with designers of the period. Its influence was so powerful that the old and somewhat dull Gothic work of Western Europe was speedily extinguished in the efforts of the bookbinder to imitate the Italian work.

The chief characteristics of the Grolier bindings are their interlaced geometrical framework, at first somewhat stiff; later he adopted the mosaic style of painting or inlaying the strapwork and filling in the spaces with graceful scroll work terminating in small outlined leaves and sprigs of conventional form, shaded with closely worked crosslines, i.e. azured. Grolier is said to have been the first collector to have his books lettered on the back; he also had the generous motto 'Io Grolierii et Amicorum' lettered on the side.

From Italy the art of bookbinding passed into France, where during the sixteenth century it was brought to great perfection.

Of the early French binders the Eve family, Du Sueil, Le Gascon, Derome, occupy the first rank, each having a characteristic style.

In England at this period much good work was done by Thomas Berthelet, Royal binder to Henry VIII; he it was who first introduced gold tooling into this country.

Chained books were common objects enough from the time of the Reformation onward, and a chained book implied a solid and heavy binding. What an old writer says makes the meaning of the chained book apparent.

'The thievish desposition of some that enter into libraries to learn no good there, hath made it necessary to secure the innocent books, even the Sacred volumes themselves, with chains— which were better deserved by those persons, who have too much learning to be hanged, and too little to be honest.'

Bookbinding shared in the general advance of the fine arts in England during the reign of Queen Elizabeth I, and the bindings of the Queen's books are superior, both as regards beauty of design and finish of workmanship, to those of her predecessors. Elizabeth was very fond of embroidered book-covers, some of which she worked with her own hands.

Charles and Samuel Mearne, binders to Charles II, did much to raise the artistic side of the craft in this country. They invented the 'Cottage' style of decoration. Many of their bindings have the fore-edge painted, under the gilt, in such a way that the work is invisible when the book is shut, and only shows when the leaves are fanned out.

Towards the end of the eighteenth century bookbinding in England was decoratively at a low level, when Roger Payne, a native of Windsor, came to London and set up as a bookbinder. He adopted a style peculiarly his own, and was the first English binder who endeavoured to make his ornaments appropriate to the character of the book on which he put them. He knew the secret that elemental forms combine best: dots, gouges, simple little circles, a crescent, and one or two sprigs of flowers made up

Plate I

Seventh-century binding of St. Cuthbert's Gospel. One of the earliest
known European bindings. *By kind permission of the Victoria and Albert
Museum.*

PLATE II

German binding, about 1485. Stamped calf with metal protective
ornamentation. *By kind permission of the Victoria and Albert Museum.*

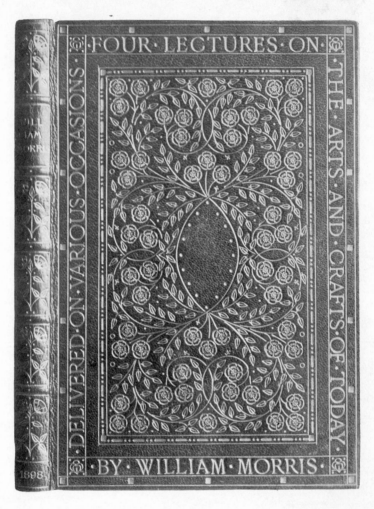

PLATE IV

Binding in green morocco with gold tooling, by J. S. Hewitt-Bates.

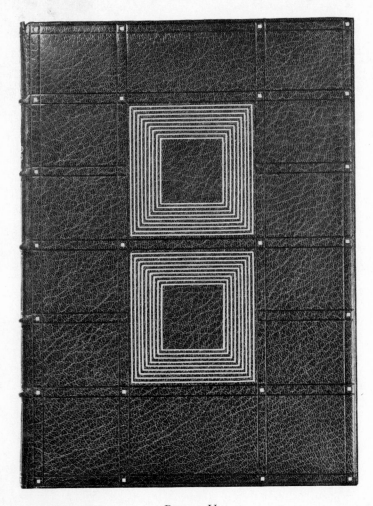

PLATE V

Binding in purple morocco with gold tooling, by George Fisher: about 1926. *By kind permission of the Victoria and Albert Museum.*

PLATE VI

Binding in blue goatskin with gold tooling, by William F. Matthews. The design is based on the Cross, with the Borough Arms of Brighton worked in detail in the central space.

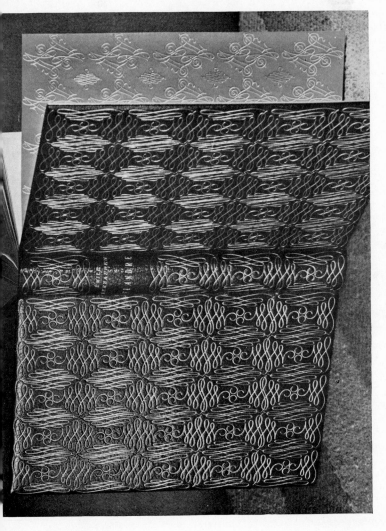

PLATE VII

Binding by Paul Bonet: Émile Verhaeren, 'Flandre'. Black levant morocco with gold tooling and doublures of red leather tooled in gold. Executed in Paris for Major J. R. Abbey during the German occupation, 1942. *By kind permission of Major Abbey.*

PLATE VIII

Student's work, Leicester College of Art. Bindings by George Allton.

the whole of his stock. But their marvellous combinations under the old craftsman's hand are the admiration of all who admire good bookbinding in the English-speaking world. He drank much and lived recklessly; but notwithstanding his irregular habits, his name ought to be respected for the work he executed. His sewing is as good now as when it left his hands more than a century ago; his backs are flexible, and his forwarding excellent. His tools, original in form, were both designed and cut by himself. His favourite leathers were russia and straight-grained morocco, which he decorated chiefly with corners and borders, and the field studded with gold dots. Even though the French school influenced him at the commencement of his career, when he became a master of his art he stood alone, original and unique.

It may be observed here, that as the mechanical aids to the art grew in number, taste declined. After Payne's time we see little else than reproduction of the great models, with often an extremely injudicious combination of different styles. The modern binder, in imitating some old master, is not able to reproduce the spirit of the original—he only betrays his own lack of invention, and his copy remains, for all his labours, the mechanical production of today.

Recent years have witnessed a marked revival in the interest in the art of bookbinding, due largely to the influence of William Morris, with whom Mr. T. J. Cobden-Sanderson was associated. They brought the art back to first principles, and their treatment shows a scholarly appreciation of ancient methods. This revival is being carried on by Mr. Douglas Cockerell and some of his pupils, and there is no doubt that the finest bookbinding in the world today is being done by English craftsmen. Two examples of such bindings are shown in the Frontispiece and Plate VI.

On the Continent a new impetus was given to bookbinding design by the work of Franz Weisse in Germany and Pierre Legrain in France. In 1917–19, Legrain's designs for the collector Jacques Doucet incorporated motifs associated with the contemporary cubist and abstract movements in art and had a great influence on French binding. Paul Bonet is recognized as the inheritor of this style, and an example of his work is shown in Plate VII.

The following is a list of works that have been referred to and quoted in the above, and further study of them will be found helpful to both teacher and student.

Historical Sketch of Bookbinding. S. T. Prideaux.

Bookbinding and the Care of Books. Douglas Cockerell. Pitman.

Bookbinding. William F. Matthews. Gollancz.

Binding, Ancient and Modern. Bell & Sons.

Bipliopegia. Hannett.

'The Development of Bookbinding Methods', by Douglas Cockerell. *The Library,* June 1932.

'Some "Cuir-Ciselé" Bookbindings in English Libraries' by E. P. Goldschmidt. *The Library,* March 1933.

'Bookbinding', *Encyclopædia Britannica,* is a well illustrated and useful article.

Bookbindings. Victoria and Albert Museum.

CHAPTER II

NECESSARY EQUIPMENT FOR THE
TEACHER OR STUDENT OF BOOKBINDING

A certain amount of permanent apparatus is absolutely necessary for any serious practice in the binding and finishing of books.

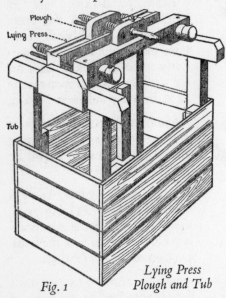

Lying Press
Plough and Tub

Fig. 1

LYING PRESS. Perhaps the most comprehensive and useful piece of equipment is the lying or cutting press. This consists of two pieces of beech 3 in. by 2¾ in. in section and 22 in. long, connected by two large screws 13½ in. apart, 1¾ in. in diameter and 2⅜ in. in diameter at the pin end, and two steel guides. On one side which is used for all purposes except cutting the cheeks are cut out. On the reverse side a groove or channel is cut to act as a guide for the plough. The plough, also of beechwood, has two cheeks which can be brought together by turning the screw handle. The left-hand cheek slides along the channel, and in the right-hand a knife is fixed by a steel holder. The knife has bevelled edges and slides in the dovetail groove of the steel holder (Fig. 1).

TUB. The lying press rests on a 'tub', a frame 2 ft. 6 in. high, 16 in. wide, and made of wood 2½ in. square (Fig. 1).

Fig. 2. Iron Nipping Press

NIPPING PRESS. An auxiliary screw or nipping press is absolutely necessary. One with a bed 18 in. by 12 in. is a convenient size, and the press must be fixed securely on a special and strong bench (*Fig. 2*). A standing press would also be found very useful (*Fig. 3*).

PRESSING BOARDS are required for use with the press. These are made of beech about 1 in. thick, and are planed perfectly smooth. Suitable sizes for use with the above apparatus are 12 in. by 8 in., and 10 in. by 6 in.

PRESSING TINS. Six of these pressing boards and six pressing tins in the same sizes would be useful for a class.

Fig. 3. Standing Press

A KNOCKING-DOWN IRON is made to fix into the lying press, and on this the cords which are laced into the boards of the book are hammered flat (*Fig. 4*).

Fig. 4. Knocking-down Iron

THE STITCHING FRAME has a flat wooden bed, at the front of which runs a slot connecting two uprights with a crossbar, which can be raised or lowered by means of wooden nuts on a screw thread cut in the uprights. For sewing, the cords are fixed on the crossbar and secured in the slot by means of keys (*Fig. 5*).

Fig. 5. Stitching Frame

CARD CUTTER. A small card cutter would be an acquisition to a school plant (*Fig. 6*), but this is a more expensive piece of equipment and is not absolutely necessary, as boards may be cut with a safety straight-edge and knife.

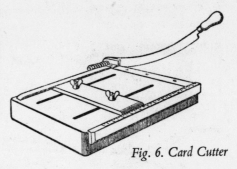

Fig. 6. Card Cutter

SMALLER APPLIANCES which are most necessary are:

Folders, which are flat pieces of bone rounded at one end and pointed at the other.

Shears or scissors with long blades.

Small tenon saw (*Fig. 7*).

Glue pot.   Paste and glue brushes.

Pair of dividers (*Fig. 8*).

Pair of Lancashire wing compasses (*Fig. 9*).

Steel set square (*Fig. 10*).

French paring knife (*Fig. 11*).

Ordinary shoemaker's knife (*Fig. 11*A).

Pair of band nippers (*Fig. 12*).

Steel scraper (*Fig. 13*).   Oil stone.

Pair of trindles (*Fig. 14*).

Backing hammer (*Fig. 15*).

Several pairs of cutting boards (*Fig. 16*).

Three pairs of backing boards (*Fig. 16*A).

Bloodstone burnisher for gilt edges (*Fig. 17*).

Gold cushion, padded and covered with rough calf (*Fig. 18*).

Gold knife (*Fig. 18*A).

The equipment described is essential for 'forwarding' a book, a term including all the processes of binding from sewing to covering. Having been covered, the book is to be 'finished', that is, lettered and decorated with blind or gold tooling. The appliances for finishing include:

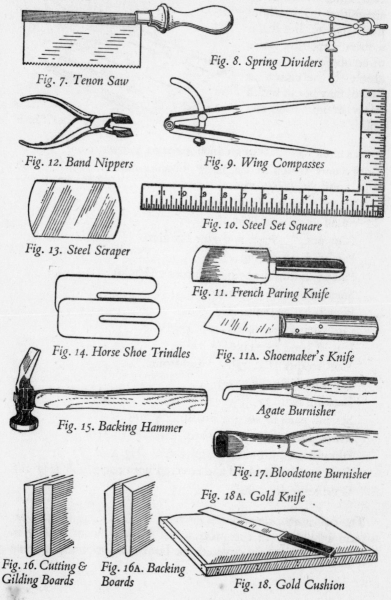

Fig. 7. Tenon Saw

Fig. 8. Spring Dividers

Fig. 12. Band Nippers

Fig. 9. Wing Compasses

Fig. 13. Steel Scraper

Fig. 10. Steel Set Square

Fig. 11. French Paring Knife

Fig. 14. Horse Shoe Trindles

Fig. 11A. Shoemaker's Knife

Fig. 15. Backing Hammer

Agate Burnisher

Fig. 17. Bloodstone Burnisher

Fig. 18A. Gold Knife

Fig. 16. Cutting & Gilding Boards

Fig. 16A. Backing Boards

Fig. 18. Gold Cushion

FINISHING PRESS. A small finishing press, which is more convenient for use than the lying press. It has two solid beech cheeks connected by a wooden screw at each end with handles for turning. A press pin is not required for screwing up a book to be finished (*Fig. 19*).

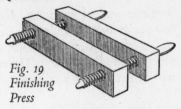

Fig. 19 Finishing Press

FILLETS. Single and two-line fillets. The fillets are brass wheels about 3½ in. in diameter, the edges of which are turned up in a lathe to one or two lines. About 1 in. is cut out of the circumference, so that in working the line may be begun and finished at a given point, as in mitreing (*see Fig. 20*).

Fig. 20. Line Fillet

GOUGES. Set of gouges, arcs of circles of different sizes cut in brass and each fitted with a wooden handle (*Fig. 21*).

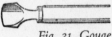

Fig. 21. Gouge

PALLETS. Set of line pallets of different lengths from ¼ in. to 1½ in. These are fitted in wooden handles and are used for working the panels of the back or sides of the book and for connecting the tools in the decoration (*Fig. 22*). They may be obtained 4 in. long with ornamental patterns cut on their slightly curved edges, and are then useful for working across the back of a book.

Fig. 22. Line Pallet

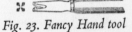

Fig. 23. Fancy Hand tool

Fig. 23A. Hand Letter

TOOLS. A selection of various tools cut in brass and fixed in wooden handles, required for making patterns to be worked in blind or gold. These may be cut and filed by the student from rods of brass ¼ in. to ½ in. in

Fig. 24. Polishing Iron

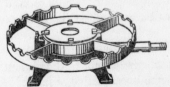

Fig. 25. Finishing Gas Stove

diameter and $3\frac{1}{2}$ in. long. The patterns, such as leaves, simple flowers and devices, are cut on one flat surface, while the other end is filed down to a point $1\frac{1}{2}$ in. in length and fixed into a wooden handle (*Fig. 23*). The cutting and designing of these tools will be dealt with in Chapter XIV.

HAND LETTERS. For extensive work, three sets of hand letters will be required. These are made like the pattern tools, but have letters and figures cut on their surfaces, each being an individual tool. A good style Roman letter should be chosen, $\frac{1}{8}$ in., $\frac{1}{4}$ in., and $\frac{3}{8}$ in. being useful sizes. All should be of the same type of letter so that they may be worked together if needed (*Fig. 23*A).

A polishing iron, which is used to give a smoothness and gloss to calf or morocco after finishing (*Fig. 24*).

A finishing stove for heating the tools (*Fig. 25*).

The gold knife and cushion as described for edge gilding, which are again needed.

Three small fine sponges.

A gold rag, which is a piece of soft woven material greased with olive oil, and is used to clean off the first superfluous gold after tooling.

A gold rubber. This may be made from best bottle rubber, cut into fine strips and soaked in petroleum, but can be obtained ready prepared from a manufacturer of bookbinders' materials.

Small folding stick or marker, ground at one end to a fine, smooth point, which is used for marking the positions of lines to be worked on the book cover.

With this equipment no bounds need be set to the progress and experiment of the student, and though the intitial outlay may seem considerable, it should be remembered that the whole of this apparatus is permanent and will require little or no replacement.

CHAPTER III

MATERIALS USED IN THE CRAFT, WITH A BRIEF DESCRIPTION OF THEIR CHARACTERISTICS

The selection of material is of vital importance to the artist, craftsman and teacher. In the school or college, as much care should be exercised in this matter as in the binder's workshop. Makeshifts and substitutes, either in plant or materials, are artistically and educationally unsound, and what, for lack of essential equipment, cannot reasonably hope to have a successful issue is better not attempted.

A simple exercise, well worked, is of the utmost value to the student, setting a standard of efficiency. The production of a piece of craft work masquerading as a fine specimen but betrayed by fundamental lack of structure, or by the use of poor and unsuitable material, is maleficent to the cause of art and craft teaching.

Papers imitating linen, linen aping leather, and leather hiding its natural beauty under some artificial and unnecessary graining, should be shunned. Each material has its characteristic texture and appropriate use, and is worthy of consideration from the point of view of its own essential worth and suitability. The student should learn to regard the sensitive choice of material as the mark of the artist craftsman, and the acceptance of the pretentious imitation as the stamp of the Philistine.

The restraint thus exercised need not limit the bookbinder in his original and experimental use of material. That there are many types of material suitable for use in bookbinding is shown in this chapter, in which only the best and most fitting for their purpose will be recommended.

PAPER. A good, but not too thick, cartridge paper, chosen to match the tone of the paper used in the book to be bound, is suitable for end-papers. For the better bound books, hand-made

C

papers may be used. Papers already coloured for end-papers or covers are available in great variety, and may be obtained in small quantities from educational suppliers of bookbinding materials. Batik papers also make pleasant covers. The student may stain or colour interesting papers in a variety of ways (*see Chapters XVII and XVIII*).

STRAWBOARDS. For the binding of the books described in the first exercise (*Chapter IV*), strawboards are quite suitable and inexpensive. These were imported chiefly from Holland. Now a very similar board of British make may be obtained in various weights and sizes. The surface size commonly used is 25 in. by 30 in., and the thickness varies according to the weight, from 8 oz. to 4 lb. a board. For school purposes a range comprising 8 oz., 12 oz., 1 lb., 1½ lb., 2 lb., would be sufficient, since other thicknesses may be made by pasting two boards together.

MILLBOARDS are of better quality than strawboards, being made from old rope fibre, and should be used for better class half-leather and full-leather bindings. These also are made in various thicknesses and sizes, from 6 p. to 10 pp. The size most suitable for school use is the 'medium' (24 in. by 19 in.), and the thicknesses 6 p., 7 p., 8 p., and 8 xx.

Strawboards and millboards may be obtained from bookbinders in small quantities or in single boards.

BOOKBINDING CLOTHS. These may be procured in great variety. They should be strong and pleasing in texture and colour. Art canvas and art vellums may also be used.

These fabrics lend themselves to various styles of decorative treatment. They may be blind or gold tooled, or stencils may be cut and worked on them with damp-proof colours.

Small patterned printed fabrics may also be used with good results for certain types of books.

LEATHERS. Many leathers are available for book covering. Those given here, in their order of merit, are recommended for their flexibility and wearing qualities and because they are generally manufactured according to the specifications of the Society of Arts.

Goat skins, when tanned, are known as moroccos. They are of three classes.

Levant morocco has a large grain. It is generally obtained from adult goats bred in South Africa. This leather is suitable for large books, and the grain is often crushed or flattened after covering by pressing between metal plates.

Niger morocco is pleasing in texture and colour. It comes from a breed of Egyptian goat and is tanned by Nigerian natives with a species of nutgall. When imported the skins are in a rough condition, but if retanned by the English manufacturer make a beautiful skin for half- or full-bound work.

Persians, which may be made either from goat or sheep, possess tensile strength, but are not recommended for their lasting qualities. They are tanned in East India with catechol tannin and are only suitable for the binding of books of an ephemeral nature. Persians are also obtained finished smooth in imitation of calf or suède.

Calf skins, if selected with care and tanned slowly with oak bark or sumach, are capable of withstanding much wear. They are beautifully soft, and, being without grain, lend themselves to delicate shades of colour in dyeing.

Seal skins, imported from Newfoundland and tanned with pyrogallol tannage, are very suitable for bookbinding. The leather is hard wearing and has a characteristic grain. It is more even in quality than many other skins.

Pig skin was used extensively in the fifteenth and sixteenth centuries for bookbinding, and has lasted well. Of late years the use of this skin has fallen into discredit through bad tannage and because of the ease with which it can be imitated. A genuine pig skin may be known by the character of the grain, showing the hair holes clearly through from the grain to the flesh side of the skin. Pig skin is used chiefly for library bindings.

Sheep skins are used for the cheaper styles of binding, but are usually grained to imitate other leathers. If properly tanned, however, such a skin may be made into a durable leather. The skins of upland breeds, such as the Welsh, are quite suitable for binding books for school use.

GOLD LEAF, ETC. The best gold leaf to use is deep English gold leaf, supplied in books of twenty-five leaves, $3\frac{1}{4}$ in. square.

Glair for finishing, or dried albumen, can be bought by the pound. It is dissolved in water to which a little vinegar is added. A few drops of milk will prevent it frothing.

It is perhaps better freshly made from the white of eggs well beaten up, diluted with half as much vinegar, and allowed to settle.

For edge gilding, Armenian bole is sold by chemists in lumps or powder form. One oz. will last quite a long time.

Thin linen or bank paper is used for mending the back of sections.

GLUE AND PASTE. Good quality hide glue in cake or powder form is used by most bookbinders. The prepared liquid glues are also good and clean in use. It is important that the glue should be of good quality.

Paste is made from wheat flour. A little cold water should be added to 2 oz. of flour and a dessert-spoonful of powdered alum, and the lumps beaten out to a smooth paste. A pint of cold water should be added before the paste is put to boil. It should be continually stirred until it boils and thickens. There are also many prepared pastes and paste powders on the market suitable for all types of this work.

CHAPTER IV

MAKING SIMPLE PORTFOLIOS AND COVERS FOR MAGAZINES, SKETCH AND NOTE BOOKS, CALENDARS AND ALBUMS

These introductory exercises may be used in junior classes as an introduction to the actual binding of books. The series will include making up unfolded sheets to form calendars, writing pads, sketch blocks, etc., and will be useful to emphasize certain points in construction and design. In this connection will be taught discrimination in proportion, kind and quality of material, and constructive and ornamental detail.

Such books as these may have paper, flexible or stiff, covers, and may be held together in various ways, the principle being that the leaves may be removed and replaced at will and the covers used again. The sheets for the leaves are selected for the purpose for which the book is to be used and the covers for the structure required.

Some ideas of methods are given, and many others will suggest themselves as the teacher or student experiments.

LACED COVERS. Books may be made with loose paper covers punched for lacings in the case of note and sketch books. The covers may be in one piece, folded squarely round the leaves, or may be strengthened by a linen hinge. Cover and leaves may be held together in a variety of ways. If by lacing, the number and spacing of the holes, and the texture and colour of the cord, give opportunity for individual taste (*Fig. 26*A and B). If rings are used they may be obtained ready made and designed to open and close (*Fig. 26*C). Punching the holes for laces and rings may be done by each student with a bradawl or punch passed round the class, and the cord threaded through with darning needles.

The decoration of the cover involves a study of the colour and texture of the paper used, and of a suitable colour scheme. It may

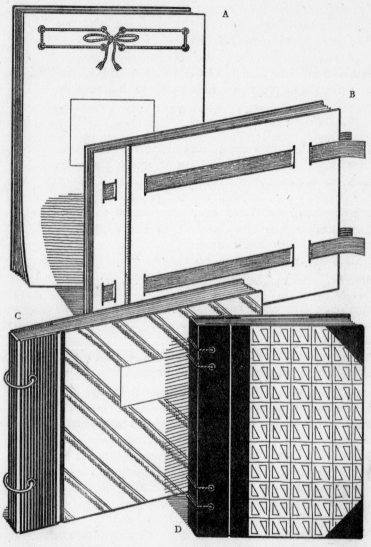

Fig. 26. A few suggestions for binding loose leaves for sketchbooks, albums, etc.

be carried out in paper cutting, stencilling, or drawing with crayon or water colour.

Where the decoration is by paper cutting, the cut-out should be laid on a sheet of well-pasted thick waste paper. Another waste sheet should be laid on top and rubbed down well with the hand so that the cut-out picks up sufficient paste on the underside. When the top sheet is removed the cut-out may be carefully lifted, placed in position on the cover, and rubbed down through another clean sheet of waste paper placed on top. By this method paste will not spread on to the cover and the cut-out will not stretch.

For sketch blocks and writing pads a more substantial cover may be desired. Boards should be used with a single or double hinge. The lower board should be in one piece to serve as a base for sketching or writing, and the front cover might be hinged. The covering material may be whole linen or part linen, or even paper with a leather hinge. Different ways of treating these are shown in Fig. 26c and D.

In these exercises attention should be directed to sound construction in the hinges, punching and lacing, good proportions and colour schemes.

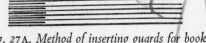

*Fig. 27A. Method of inserting guards for books
made up of single leaves*

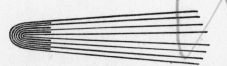

*Fig. 27B. Method of inserting guards for books
made up of folded leaves*

Books may be made to hold pictures or press notices, and to allow for this a guard about 1 in. wide and of a thickness equal to whatever will be inserted, is placed between each leaf, level with the back edge, punched and laced through. In this case, however, both back and front boards should be hinged (*Fig. 27*A).

READING CASES for school magazines and weekly papers will make a useful exercise for students.

Two mill or strawboards should first be cut about ⅜ in. larger all round than the size of the magazine the case is to hold. These may be covered in whole linen or half-leather, i.e. leather back and corners with linen or paper sides.

Before covering, a strip of board must be cut ½ in. to 1 in. wide, according to the thickness of the magazine, and used as a gauge between the two boards.

If the case is to be covered in whole linen a piece must be cut out large enough to turn in 1 in. all round, allowing for the gauge between the boards. When this has been glued evenly all over with thin glue, the left-hand board is placed on the linen, leaving the inch to turn in at top and bottom and at the left side. The cardboard gauge is placed up to this board and the right-hand board is placed down in position quite level at the head, so that it comes exactly opposite the left-hand board. The gauge is removed and each corner of the linen cut at an angle of 45 degrees, leaving the thickness of the board beyond the corner (*Fig. 28*).

The linen is turned in at head and tail, and tucked in at the mitres with the thumbnail or folder. The right and left sides should be turned in, seeing that the corners meet evenly and that no rough edges of the linen are sticking out at the extreme corners. The edges of the boards should be rubbed square, the case turned over and the linen rubbed down to the boards evenly all over.

It is most important that the whole of this process should be as speedy as possible. Should the glue be allowed to set before the linen is rubbed to the board it will be difficult to make it stick.

A strip of linen like that used for the cover, 2 in. wider than the gauge and about ¼ in. less than the length of the board, should now be glued down to the joint on the inside of the case, rubbing it well down with the folder so that it sticks to joint and boards. Two sheets of coloured or white paper, ¼ in. smaller than the board all round, should be cut and pasted on the inside of each board.

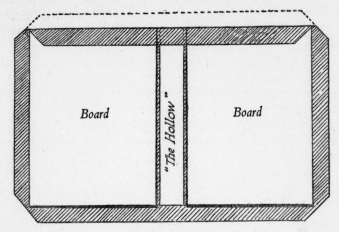

Fig. 28. Method of making cloth case

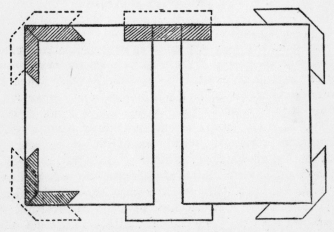

Fig. 29. Method of making half bound case

Holes should be punched at the head and tail of the joint and eyelets inserted and clinched. A cord is then tied through the holes so that the magazine may be inserted and held in position while read.

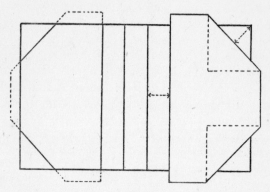

Fig. 30. Method of cutting out sides and showing proportion of back to corners

Such a reading case may be made in half-leather. Back and covers must be cut out of the leather chosen in correct proportion. A case to hold one monthly part of *The Studio* would have boards 8½ in. by 12¼ in., and ¾ in. might be left between them for the back or joint. In this case the leather would be cut to allow 1½ in. on the boards on either side of the joint, in addition to the space between the boards, making the leather back 3¾ in. wide and 13¾ in. long, which allows ¾ in. to turn in at the top and bottom. To be in correct proportion to the back the corners should be cut out so that they measure 1¾ in. across the diagonal of the corner after ¾ in. has been turned in on two sides. Four corners are needed. When cut out the back and corners should be pared evenly on the edges for about ⅛ in. (*see Chapter XIII*).

The four corners are pasted and left in pairs, pasted sides together, to soak. They are put on the boards first. Each piece should be placed on a corner of the board, allowing the leather to come beyond the corner the thickness of the board. The top side should be turned in and the projecting bit should be tucked in with the folder and the side overlap turned in. The mitres must be even at the corners and the leather stuck squarely to the board. Each corner should be treated in this manner and then the back put on. The back should be well pasted and left doubled over to soak. When pliable it should be opened out, the gauge placed down the centre and a board at either side. The gauge is removed and the leather turned in at the top and the bottom. If the case is to have a leather joint inside, this is cut out to reach about ½ in. over on to each board and about ¼ in. less at the head and tail. It must be well pasted and placed on the joint and well rubbed down.

The sides may be of linen or paper, and must be cut out to fit just over the paring at the back and corners (*Figs. 29* and *30*).

When the sides have been glued on and turned in, the inside of the case should be lined with white or tinted paper, leaving ¼ in. margin all round on both boards. Flaps and ties should be fixed before the lining paper is put on.

Other styles of case will suggest themselves in full linen or vellum, with tape or silk ribbon ties threaded through by making holes with ½ in chisel after the case has been made and lined in (*Fig. 31*).

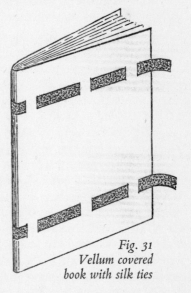

Fig. 31
Vellum covered
book with silk ties

From these exercises the making of more elaborate cases and portfolios to hold drawings will develop, and the ingenuity and invention of the teacher or student will be called into play in their individual design.

CHAPTER V

BINDING A SINGLE SECTION BOOK:
SEWING, CUTTING AND COVERING

In this early exercise the book chosen may be printed or of plain paper for manuscript. For the manuscript or notebook, a plain sheet may be folded into a sixteen-page section in the manner described in Chapter VI. The printed section may be folded from a sixteen-page sheet, or may be a section already folded. In the latter case the stitches must be cut and the cover removed.

ONE SECTION BOOKS. The most elementary exercise is to fold the paper and cut the edges of the leaves before sewing, and then to sew into a paper cover ⅛ in. larger at the head, tail and fore-edge. For the older student this simple exercise might be omitted, and the procedure will then be as follows:

The section being folded, two sheets of paper to tone with the paper of the book should be folded round for end-papers, and a strip of thin linen or muslin, 1½ in. wide and the length of the book, pasted round the fold to strengthen the section.

To facilitate this process when a class is working the exercise, a number of strips might be placed on a sheet of glass or a wooden board which has been well pasted, and rubbed down over a sheet of waste paper. The board might then be passed round the class. Each child would take a strip, fold it lengthwise down the centre, open it out, place the back of the book to the fold, draw the strip of linen firmly over and smooth it down.

The next stage is sewing. Three or five holes, according to the size of the book, may be made. The printed book allows of individual treatment with regard to the spacing of the holes with reference to the letterpress. This gives an exercise in artistic judgement of proportion. In the plain sheet the holes may be spaced equally. The needle is put from the inside of the section through the middle hole A, through the next hole below B, into the middle of the section again, and out through the top hole C, bringing the thread over the centre hole. The needle must now be taken to the outside of the section and in again through the centre, where the two ends are tied in a double knot across the middle thread, and the ends cut off about ¼ in. from the knot. For sewing, see Fig. 32.

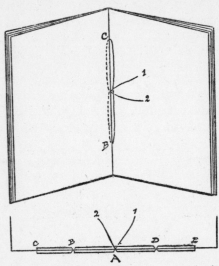

*Fig. 32. Method of sewing one section books
three and five holes*

The leaves must then be cut. Pencil lines should be drawn round the book, making the angles absolutely true, and if press and plough are not obtainable a safety straight-edge and sharp pointed knife may be used.

Boards should be cut ⅛ in. larger than the book at head, tail and fore-edge. For this 8 oz. strawboard will probably be most suitable (*see Chapter III on Materials*).

The covering may be of paper, decorated or plain, or of linen. Chapters XVII and XVIII are devoted to methods of staining and decorating paper.

The boards must be placed ¼ in. from the back of the book, and a strip of paper cut the length of the boards and wide enough to cover the fold up to the boards. This is called the hollow and acts as a gauge. The cover, linen or paper, is placed flat on the table, and on this must be placed the two boards with the gauge between. The cover is then cut with ¾ in. to turn in all round (*Fig. 28*).

Croid, or some other liquid glue, is perhaps preferable to hot glue for use in schools. This must not be too thick and be brushed evenly on to the cover, working from the centre and off the edges. All lumps or bristles should be removed. One board must be placed ¾ in. from the left side of the cover, the gauge or hollow placed up to this, and the other board laid beside it and level with

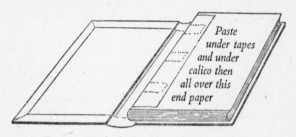

Paste
under tapes
and under
calico then
all over this
end paper

*Fig. 33. Method of pasting down case book
which has not been backed*

the head of, and parallel to, the first board. The corners are then cut off at an angle of 45 degrees, leaving a margin beyond the board equal to its thickness. The material must then be turned in at the head and tail with the aid of a folder, and care taken to press the material tightly over the edge of the boards. The overlap at the fore-edge is next turned in, tucking in the corner with the folder in order to make an even mitre.

The case thus made is turned over and the cover rubbed carefully down to the boards, using the folder or the hand over a sheet of waste paper.

The process is performed more quickly than it can be described, and should be as speedy as possible, so that the cover is neatly turned in before the glue sets. It may be noted that cold glue does not set as quickly as hot.

The cover must now be folded down the centre of the back and then opened flat, the underside of the book pasted and the book laid on the right-hand board, leaving ⅛ in. squares at the edges. The front of the book is pasted and the other board pulled over to coincide exactly with the lower board (*Fig. 33*). The book should be put between wooden pressing boards, and placed in the nipping press for a minute or two, and then taken out and opened to ascertain that the end-papers are sticking securely. If the covering has been successful the book should again be placed in the press with light pressure, or left under a weight until perfectly dry. Unless this is done the boards will warp and refuse to lie flat.

A variety of treatments lend themselves to the final decoration of the cover.

HALF- OR QUARTER-BOUND BOOKS. A further exercise on similar lines is to bind the book in half or quarter linen or paper.

For the half-bound book corners are cut as shown in Fig. 32. The size of corners and back, which are of different material from that used for the sides, is determined by the proportions of the book. The width of the back piece is equal to the vertical of the triangular corner (*Fig. 30*).

A corner must be carefully glued and the board placed on it, leaving equal margins for turning in on each side. These margins should be turned in and mitred in the same way as the corners of the full linen book (*Fig. 28*).

The four corners are put on in this manner. When the back is cut the required width and length it should be glued, the gauge put down the centre, and the boards put down on either side. The gauge should then be removed and the material turned in at the head and tail.

Care must be taken that corners and back are glued to the same surface of the board.

The sides may be of paper of a suitable colour and texture, or of a differently coloured linen. If leather is thought more suitable, a thin skiver or sheep might be substituted for back and corners.

The sides should be cut to allow for ¾ in. turning in with a straight-edge to go along the back, and should be placed on the side of the board to cover the edge of the material on the back by about ⅛ in. The two corners of the side should be turned over at an angle of 45 degrees, the top edge lying parallel with the back as in Fig. 33, and should overlap the corners already covered by ⅛ in. The side must be tried on both boards before the corners are finally cut off, and when this is done both sides may be cut together. To cut, put a straight-edge by the fold and cut with a knife along the crease.

The sides must be glued, keeping the right side of the material perfectly clean, placed in position on the boards and well rubbed down, reversed, and the material turned in all the way round. The end-papers are then pasted down and the book placed in the press, as before described (*Fig. 33*).

If the colours and materials of such a binding are well chosen the book will present a pleasing and interesting appearance. The title may be written on a paper label and stuck on the front cover towards the head.

CHAPTER VI

THE FOLDING OF BOOKS IN SHEETS:
TREATMENT OF THE ALREADY BOUND
BOOK AND MENDING

The first process in the binding of a book is the folding of the sheets. If received from the printer the sheets are flat as they leave the printing machine, and the pages are so 'imposed' that when properly folded they will follow consecutively and have equal margins.

SIZES OF BOOKS. The various sizes of books are named according to the number of leaves into which the sheet is folded—as folio (folded once, two leaves), quarto (folded twice into four leaves), octavo, eight leaves, 12mo, 16mo, 32mo, etc. It must be understood, however, that the individual size of each of these is governed by the size of the original sheet on which the book is printed.

A few of the most usual sizes are given here:

	Half or Folio	Quarto	Octavo
Imperial	30″ × 22″	22″ × 15″	15″ × 11″	11″ × 7½″
Royal	25″ × 20″	20″ × 12½″	12½″× 10″	10″ × 6¼″
Demy	22½″× 17½″	17½″× 11¼″	11¼″× 8¾″	8¾″ × 5⅝″
Crown	20″ × 15″	15″ × 10″	10″ × 7½″	7½″× 5″
Foolscap	17″ × 13½″	13½″× 8½″	8½″× 6¾″	6¾″× 4¼″
Double Crown 30″× 20″		Double Pott 25″× 15	Pott 15″× 12½″

THE OCTAVO. The most usual size into which a sheet is folded is the octavo or 16-page. The first 16 pages are imposed by the printer as in Fig. 34. The next section would consist of pages 17 to 32, the signature being 'C' on page 17. Section D would be 33 to 48.

D

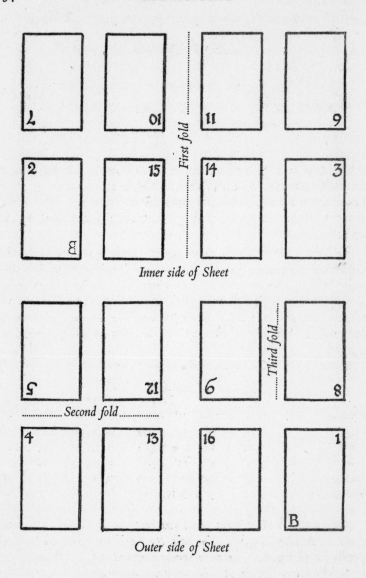

Fig. 34. Method of folding octavo sheet

SIGNATURES are the letters or numbers placed by the printer at the foot of the first page of each sheet, to guide the binder in the making up or collating of the book. J, V and W are letters generally omitted. The first sheet of the text is usually B. Sheet A consists of the title-page, preface, etc.

FOLDING. An octavo sheet of any size is folded in this manner.

The sheets to be folded are placed on the bench, with the signature on the outer side of the section face downwards, and the signature on the first page under the left hand. Taking a folder in the right hand, the right-hand side of the sheet is brought over so that pages 3 and 6 fall exactly over 2 and 7. This is attained by holding the section up against the light so that it is possible to see that the printed pages coincide, or by bending the corner over the folder so that the figures of each page may be seen and placed exactly over one another. When this has been done, the pages are held in position by the left hand and the fold creased with the bone folder.

This brings pages 4–13 and 5–12 uppermost. The top part of the sheet is then brought down with the left hand so that pages 5 and 12 fall exactly over pages 4 and 13, and the section is again creased with the folder. This brings the centre of the section, pages 8 and 9, to the top. Page 9 is brought over level with 8, forming the third fold and completing the section (*Fig. 34*).

Some papers crease badly when the third fold is brought over. To avoid this it is well, before making the third fold, to slit the head of the sheet at the second fold just past the centre with the folder.

The same principles govern the folding of most sections. Folio has one fold only, quarto two folds, octavo three folds, 16mo four folds.

BOUND AND CASED BOOKS. A book is said to be 'bound' when the bands on which the book is sewn are laced into the boards and actually become part of the binding.

A book is 'cased' when the cover has been made apart from the book and only held to the book by the mull and end-papers being pasted on to the boards.

The book, which has previously been bound or cased, must be taken to pieces or 'pulled' before re-binding. In the bound book the bands or cords which have been laced into the boards must be cut and the boards detached.

REMOVING LEATHER. When the leather is removed from the back of a flexible binding the glue will sometimes come with it, leaving the back clear, but if the leather or lining paper adhere firmly to the back, it is better to screw up the book in the lying press and paste the whole of the back over with thin paste, leaving it to soak until the softened leather or paper can be scraped off with a folder or dull knife. Care must be taken not to weaken the paper at the back. The backs of the sections will now be exposed. The paste should be cleaned off with paper shavings. In a sixteen-page section four leaves should be counted; the sewing threads in the centre will then be seen. These threads should be cut, another four leaves counted and, the next signature being brought to view, the section should be held firmly and pulled from the book. Each section should be treated in the same manner, any glue removed from the back of each, and the sections kept in the proper order.

A case book will be pulled to pieces in the same way, but the boards are more easily detached by cutting the mull and end-papers if they have not already broken away with wear.

KNOCKING OUT THE JOINT. If the book has been 'backed', that is, if a groove has been made on either side into which the board fits, and which is called a joint, this backing must now be knocked out. For this, the knocking-down iron is screwed up in the lying press. A few sections are taken at a time, kept level at the back, and tapped gently down the crease with a smooth, round-faced hammer. The sections are then turned over and the crease hammered on the reverse side.

MENDING. When the sections are all straightened, any weak or torn sections must be mended. Usually the first and last sections will need repairing at the back. A number of strips of thin linen or bank paper, about $\frac{1}{2}$ in. wide and the length of the book, should be cut, a piece of glass or board well pasted, and the number of strips required laid down. A sheet of waste paper should be placed over them and rubbed well down with the hand so that the strips pick up the paste. They should be lifted up one at a time and placed straight on a thin sheet of paper. A torn section should be placed half over a strip, rubbed down with the forefinger, and the other half of the strip brought over the section by lifting up the sheet of paper and rubbing it down again on the section (*Fig. 35*). This will be found a neat and clean way of mending. Plates and any loose leaves must be attached to a section in a like manner.

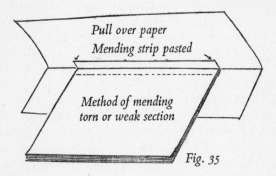

Pull over paper
Mending strip pasted

Method of mending
torn or weak section

Fig. 35

If any page is torn across the print or margin, the overlapping edges must be carefully pasted together and a piece of transparent Japanese or tissue paper placed on either side. The page is then placed between blotting-paper to dry. When dry the tissue paper is torn off, leaving a slight film on either side of the tear.

PRESSING. When all sections and repaired pages are dry the book should be well pressed. To do this several sections should be knocked up level at back and head and placed between pressing tins and boards. More sections should be placed just above the others, but with their backs the reverse way. The whole book is built up in this manner and put in the nipping or standing press. Care must be taken that it is put under the middle of the screw, or the pressing will be uneven. A heavy pressure should be put on the book for at least one hour, when it should be ready for the next process of binding.

CHAPTER VII

THE BOOK SEWN ON TAPES OR CORDS
FOR CASE WORK OR SPLIT BOARDS

COLLATING. The book which has been taken to pieces and mended, as described in the previous chapter, is now taken out of press and collated to ensure that sheets and plates are in order. The book is held in the right hand at the top right-hand corner and fanned out with the left hand. As each section is released the signature may be seen. Signatures at the bottom of each section should follow consecutively. J, V and W are generally omitted as signatures, and if the number of sections is greater than twenty-three the signatures are doubled—as AA or 2A, BB or 2B.

If the end-papers are to be sewn round the first and last sections the book is now ready for sewing. The manuscript or notebook must be sewn on tapes; a letterpress book may be sewn on tapes or cords.

A book to be sewn on tapes must first be marked for the position and number of tapes. Three is the usual number for an octavo book, four for a quarto, and five for folio (*Fig. 36*).

KETTLE STITCHES. The book is knocked up level to the head and back. The position of the kettle stitches is marked by a line $\frac{1}{2}$ in. to $\frac{3}{4}$ in. from each end. For an octavo book on three tapes the position of the middle tape should be marked exactly in the centre, and then the positions of the tapes on either side. These should be slightly nearer to the kettle stitches than to the middle tape. If the book is kept level at the head and the sections slightly fanned out the marks may be made across the back with a pencil and ruler (*Fig. 36*). The tapes for a book of this size will be $\frac{1}{2}$ in. wide, thin and slightly stiffened, but strips may be cut from offcuts of the linen used for covering the books. Each tape is cut 2 in. longer than the width of the book.

SAWING-IN. If the book to be sewn is letterpress the kettle stitches at head and tail are often sawn in. This is done by placing pressing boards at either side of the book, $\frac{1}{2}$ in. below the back, and, with a tenon saw, making a cut across $\frac{1}{16}$ in. deep on the marks at the head and tail. When the kettle stitch is made it sinks into the saw marks in each section.

Before sewing, in this early exercise, it is, perhaps, well to make holes with the needle through each pencil mark, by opening the section and pushing the needle through from the back. This ensures neat and careful sewing.

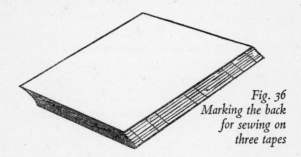

Fig. 36
Marking the back
for sewing on
three tapes

SEWING. The first section is placed face downwards on the bench, back towards the sewer, and head to the right. The left hand is placed inside the section and, with the right hand, the threaded needle is pushed through the kettle stitch at the head. The left hand should receive the needle and pass it from the inside into the next hole made, leaving an end of about 2 in. of thread hanging outside at the kettle stitch. The needle is again taken in the right hand, the first tape placed in position, and the thread taken across and through the third hole, out of the fourth hole, across the second tape, in at the fifth hole, out of the sixth and across the third tape. It is now passed through the seventh hole and out of the eighth, which is the tail kettle stitch. The thread should be pulled tightly but parallel with the section, so that the strain is not on the paper.

The second section must be placed on top of the first and the thread passed through the tail kettle stitch and up to the head, working reversely. When the thread is brought out at the head kettle stitch it must be fastened by a knot to the end left for the purpose. Another section is laid on and sewn from right to left in the same manner.

When the kettle stitch is reached it must be fastened to the section below by a 'catch-up' stitch. This is made by passing the needle between the two sections below, bringing it out at the end of the book, through the loop in the thread (*Fig. 39*), and drawing the thread taut, pulling it upwards. If the mark has been sawn, in, the knot should rest in the saw mark.

All sections are sewn on in this manner and the thread of the last section fastened off twice to make the sewing secure. The thread should be cut off at a distance of $\frac{1}{2}$ in. from the book, and this end is rubbed in between the sections when the book is glued up. If the book consists of many sections they may be caught up in groups as in diagram (*Fig. 42*).

If end-papers have not been sewn on they must now be cut out and stuck on. For this class of work two sheets of cartridge or other strong paper which matches the book are cut double the size of the book and folded down the centre. They are then pasted down the folded edges about $\frac{1}{8}$ in., and placed up to the back edges of the book on either side. It is better that the end-papers should be a little over the back than under, to give additional play in the joint when the book is pasted down. The book should be placed between pressing boards, put under a weight, and left till the paste is dry.

If the book is letterpress, and to be sewn on cords, the positions of the cords must be marked. The most convenient method is to screw the book up in the lying press, as was described for the sawing-in of the kettle stitches (*Fig. 37*), but in this case the marks for cords may also be sawn in. Three cords will be sufficient for an octavo book. The kettle stitch marks at head and tail are sawn in first, then the position of the middle cord, and last the cord marks on either side, which should be slightly nearer the kettle stitches than the middle cord—as in the position of tapes. The saw marks must only be deep enough to pierce the middle sheet of each section.

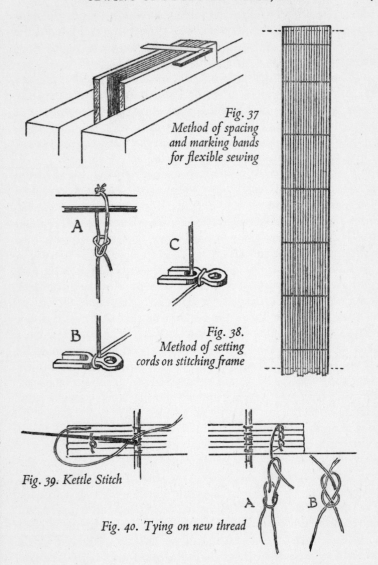

Fig. 37
Method of spacing
and marking bands
for flexible sewing

A

C

B

Fig. 38.
Method of setting
cords on stitching frame

Fig. 39. Kettle Stitch

Fig. 40. Tying on new thread

A

B

SETTING-UP ON THE STITCHING FRAME. The cords must now be set up on the stitching frame. The book is placed on the bed of the frame with its back towards the worker and its head to the right. Three cords must be secured by a simple reef knot to the loops of cord tied round the top beam of the frame (*Fig. 38*A). They must be cut to come about 6 in. below the bed and secured by means of keys supplied for that purpose. The key is taken in the right hand, the cord pulled down by the left, the key is placed to the left of the cord, which is wrapped once round the waist of the key, and the key turned over so that the main cord slips between the prongs. The key is then slipped through the slot in the bed of the frame, keeping the prongs away from the worker (*Fig. 38*B and *38*C).

The other cords are fixed in the same way and made to correspond with the saw marks in the book. They must be kept perfectly perpendicular and made taut by the use of the screws under the beam (*Fig. 41*). It will be found convenient to place the cords to the right-hand side of the frame, as this will allow the left arm, when sewing, to be on the inside of the frame.

The book should now be taken from the frame and placed at the right-hand side, with the head to the left and the first signature or section on the top. This should be placed face downwards on the bed of the stitching frame, so that the saw marks fit the cords.

SEWING. The left hand should be held in the centre of the section and the threaded needle put through the head saw mark, brought out on the right-hand side of the first cord, passed across the cord and inserted again through the same hole, but on the other side of the cord. This is repeated for each cord and the thread is finally brought out at the tail kettle stitch. The thread is pulled taut so that each cord settles into the saw cuts. (*Fig. 44*). The second section is put on and worked from left to right, the kettle stitches being made in the manner described for sewing on tapes.

SWELL. When a few sections have been sewn they should be knocked down by tapping between the cords with a piece of wood or a small pressing board used edgeways. This will reduce the 'swell' which is caused by the thread passing along each

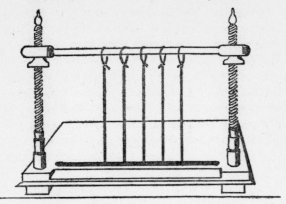

Fig. 41. Stitching frame set for sewing

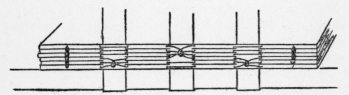

Fig. 42. Sewing on tapes

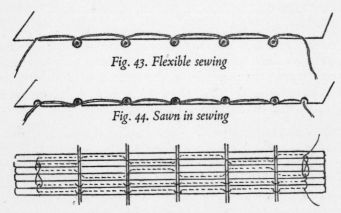

Fig. 43. Flexible sewing

Fig. 44. Sawn in sewing

Fig. 45. Sewing two sheets on

section. In order to avoid too great a swell, thick books consisting of many thin sections are sewn 'two sheets on' (*Fig. 45*). The first two sections are sewn all along in the manner described, but when the third section is placed on, the needle is passed through the kettle stitch and inside the section to the first cord. Then the fourth section is placed on and the thread passed across the cord and inserted in the saw mark of section four. It is brought out from the fourth section at the second cord, and put in again in the third section at the other side of the cord. After crossing the third cord

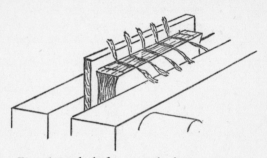

Fig. 46. Method of screwing book up in press for knocking out swell

and entering the fourth section it is passed through the kettle stitch of the fourth section and is fastened between the first two sections. In this way the thread only passes once along the two sections. Folders placed in the middle of the sections will save inconvenience. Each two sections are treated in the same manner, but the last two are sewn all along as the first two.

THE WEAVER'S KNOT (*Fig. 40*). The usual knot for tying one thread to another as the work proceeds is the weaver's knot. The end of the broken strand is placed across the end of the new strand from left to right, and both held at the crossing point between the thumb and finger of the left hand. With the right hand the long portion of the new strand is passed over the thumb, behind its short end and in front of the broken end. The broken end is bent down over it and under the loop resting on the thumb. The knot is tightened by pulling the new strand. The threads should be joined as near the back as possible so that the knot is only drawn through a saw mark once and rests in the middle of the section.

Considerable judgement is required in the choice of thread and the method of sewing to govern the swell. If the swell is too great the book becomes unmanageable in rounding; if too little, it will be difficult to back. A medium grade thread is required for sound work in the subsequent processes. Before glueing up the book should be examined, and if the swell is too great it may be reduced. The book should be knocked up level to the back and head,

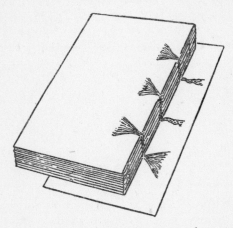

Fig. 47. Scraping of slips on a tin and pasting them on to the side of book

and placed on a pressing board with slips or tapes between the pressing board and the book on the left-hand side. Board and book are then lowered into the lying press, keeping the board about $\frac{1}{2}$ in. above the back of the book. The press is screwed up tightly, and the right side of the book beaten against the pressing board with a hammer and the strings or tapes pulled tight.

This will greatly reduce the swell (*Fig. 46*).

If end-papers have not been sewn on they must be pasted on in the manner described earlier in the chapter.

CORDS. The cords should now be frayed out. The strands should be parted, a piece of tin placed between the cords and the book, and the strands should be scraped with a knife to flatten them out in a fan shape. They should be cut off with the shears about 1 in. from the back and drawn through the thumb and finger with a little paste. They may then be stuck down to the end-papers on either side of the book, rubbing them down with a folder, and making them lie as flat as possible (*Fig. 47*).

N.B.—The above method of 'sawn in' sewing is only recommended for the sewing of books which are to be put in publishers' cases. The fact of having saw cuts across the back prevents the leaves being opened right up to the fold.

For best work 'flexible' sewing is recommended, and will be described in Chapter XI.

CHAPTER VIII

GLUEING-UP, ROUNDING, CUTTING, MAKING CASE AND PASTING DOWN

The book sewn on tapes or cords is now ready for glueing-up. It should be taken between both hands and the back and head knocked up against the lying press till all the sections are perfectly level and square. Held tightly in the left hand, it should be lowered into the press until the back is about 3 in. above the cheeks of the press, which should then be screwed up tightly with the hand. A small brush should be charged with hot, thin glue and rubbed all over the back, the glue being worked well between the sections with the fingers or a folder, but kept from soiling the end-papers (*Fig. 48*).

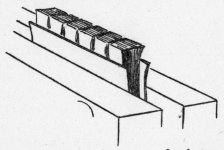

Fig. 48. Book screwed up in press for glueing-up

Glueing-up is an important process and must be done with great care. If the glue applied is too thick it will not run between the sections; if it is too thin it will run too far between and spoil the book.

When the book is taken out of the press it should be laid on a pressing board to dry, with the back projecting slightly over the board. Care must be taken that the book is not twisted in any way as any fault will be found impossible to remedy when once the glue is dry.

The binding or casing of the book sewn on tapes is taken first, i.e. the manuscript or sketch book.

CUTTING THE FORE-EDGE. When the 'glueing-up' is almost dry the fore-edge may be cut. From the back edge of the book the amount to be cut off should be marked with compasses at the head and tail, and a line drawn through the points made (*Fig. 49*). Two cutting boards are required (*Fig. 16*). One, the cut against, is placed level with the edge of the book on the left-hand side, with a waste strip of strawboard between board and book to prevent cutting the wooden board. The other cutting board, the runner, is placed just up to the pencilled cutting line. Book and boards are lifted carefully with the left hand and lowered into the press until the runner is perfectly level with the cheek of the press. The press should be screwed up tightly with the press pin and equal pressure obtained by keeping the cheeks of the press parallel with each other.

Fig. 49. Method of marking fore-edge for cutting with plough

During the process of putting the book in the press it must be kept perfectly square, or an uneven cut will result.

The plough should be placed on the press so that it will run along the channel cut in the cheek of the press, and should be held by both hands, the left on the screw and the right on the handle. The screw is turned till the knife touches the runner board, and the plough is then moved backwards and forwards, turning the screw slightly each time the plough is pushed forward. If the knife is correctly sharpened a true and smooth cut should result.

If the book is to be left with a flat back, as in the case of a very

thin book, the head and tail are cut in the same manner; the
amount to be cut off is marked by placing a set-square level with
the back. When the book is placed in the press for cutting, the
back should always be towards the worker.

ROUNDING. If, however, the book is to be rounded, this is
done before the head and tail are cut.

The book is laid on the press with the fore-edge towards the
worker, and the back drawn over by the left hand while the
thumb is kept on the fore-edge. The back is then tapped gently
with the hammer. The book is turned over and the process repeated. This is done until the back assumes an even convex form
which should be part of a circle (*Fig. 51*).

Rounding should be done
while the glue on the back is
still elastic enough to avoid
cracking between the sections.

The head and tail of the
book are next cut (*Fig. 63*).

CUTTING THE BOARDS.
After this process a pair of
boards should be cut. For an
octavo book 1 lb. or 1½ lb.
strawboard will be appro-
priate in thickness. The boards
must be cut perfectly true and
square, leaving about ⅛ in.
'square' projecting beyond the

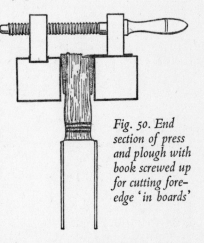

Fig. 50. End
section of press
and plough with
book screwed up
for cutting fore-
edge 'in boards'

edges of the book after the boards have been placed ¼ in. away
from the back edge of the book (as shown in Fig. 33).

A piece of muslin or linen, ¼ in. less than the length of the back
and 2 in. wider than the width of the back, should be cut. The
back of the book should be glued and the mull placed on in position and well rubbed down with a folder (*Fig. 33*). A piece of
paper is then cut exactly the size of the back of the book and glued
on to the back over the mull and well rubbed down. This is called
'the liner'. Another strip of paper is cut, the width of the back but

E

the length of the boards, i.e. slightly longer than the book. This is called 'the hollow'.

COVERING. The linen for the cover should be cut to allow ¾ in. for turning in all round. The piece should be placed on a waste sheet of paper and glued evenly all over with thin glue, removing all lumps or bristles. The boards should be placed on either side of the book and knocked up level with the tail, allowing the ⅛ in. square at the fore-edges and ¼ in. away from back. Book and board should be placed down on to the glued cover

Fig. 51. Method of Rounding

¾ in. away from the edge of the linen on each side. With the boards held in position the hollow already cut should be placed on the cover up to the back (*Fig. 52*). The other half of the linen is then drawn over and rubbed down to the top board. The boards are opened flat and the book taken away. The corners of the linen should be cut off at an angle of 45 degrees, leaving the thickness of the board beyond the corner. With a folder the linen at the head and tail should be turned over the boards and rubbed down. The corners are then tucked in and the fore-edges turned over. The case should be turned over and the linen rubbed down so that it sticks to the boards. This part of the process has already been described at greater length in Chapter V (*Fig. 28, p. 25*).

A case has now been made into which the book should fit with ⅛ in. squares all round. The book should be placed front upwards on the underneath board and the top board drawn over so that the linen cover comes tightly over the back of the book. With the point of the folder a groove should be rubbed down the edge of the boards on either side of the back. If there is no artificial grain stamped on the linen used for the cover it may now be pasted down. The top board is opened, care being taken that the squares of the lower board are equal. Paste should be applied underneath the tapes, and then on top of them. The mull should be laid

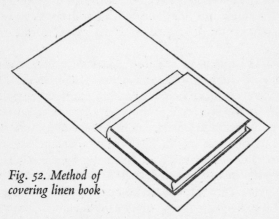

Fig. 52. Method of covering linen book

down and pasted, and then all over the end-paper, taking the brush from the centre off all the edges. The top board is closed on to the pasted end-paper and the book turned over. Keeping the squares even, the other end-paper should be pasted down in the same manner (*Fig. 33, p. 30*). The book should be placed between pressing boards, given a nip and left in for a few minutes. Then the book should be taken out of press and each cover opened to allow the air to get to the end-papers. If all is well with the book it is again placed in the press and left there till dry. If it is not possible to keep the book in press it should be allowed to dry under a heavy weight, or the boards will not lie flat.

The process described in this exercise applies only to manuscript and sketch books, or thin letterpress books which are not 'backed'.

CHAPTER IX

THE LIBRARY BINDING IN SPLIT BOARDS, BACKING, FRENCH JOINTS AND ZIG-ZAG END-PAPERS

If a stronger or more durable style of binding is required for school reading or library books, the tapes on which the books are sewn may be stuck into split boards. This will constitute a bound book as opposed to the cased book described in the previous exercise.

The book is brought on as before, but with zig-zag end-papers, and is sewn on tapes or strips of vellum, not on cords. The zig-zag end-papers are made in the following manner: Four sheets of good white or toned cartridge and two sheets of coloured paper are cut out so that when folded they are about $\frac{1}{2}$ in. wider than the book and the same length. They are all folded in half, and two white sheets are well pasted $\frac{1}{8}$ in. down the folded edge, and the two coloured sheets are stuck fold to fold on the pasted edge of each (*Fig. 53A*). They should be placed between pressing boards to dry. When the paste is dry, Sheet 1 is folded over the coloured or paste down paper (*Fig. 53B*), and the other white sheet (1A) is folded the reverse way, forming the zig-zag (*Fig. 53C*). The other folded sheet of white is inserted into this, and when put on the book the sewing passes through the loose inserted sheet.

This form of end-paper is preferable to those stuck on. Being sewn on, there is no strain thrown on the first and last sections in opening and closing the boards, and it allows each leaf to open right up to the back. When sewn, glued up, cut and rounded, as described in Chapter VIII, the book has now to be backed, i.e. a groove has to be made into which the boards will fit, helping to keep the back in its convex form.

BACKING BOARDS. For this purpose a pair of backing boards a little longer than the book are required (*Fig. 16A*). The book is

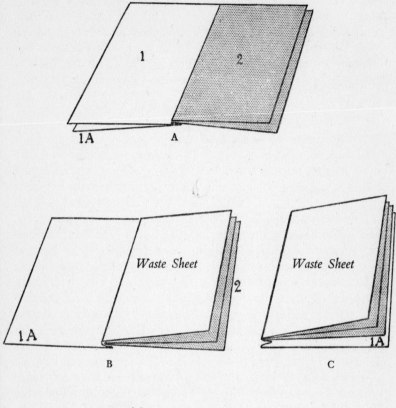

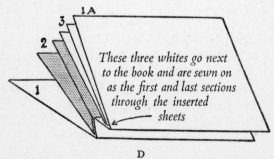

Fig. 53. The making of zig-zag end-papers

placed on the lying press, back towards the worker. A backing board is laid a short distance away from the edge of the back on top of the tapes. The book and board are turned over and the other backing board is placed to correspond with the first. The distance of the backing boards from the edge of the back is governed by the thickness of the boards to be used for the book.

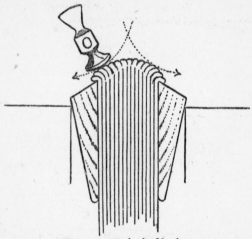

Fig. 54. Method of backing

Boards and book are gripped firmly in the left hand and carefully lowered into the press, keeping their positions unaltered until the outer edges of the backing boards are about ¼ in. above the cheeks of the press. The press is screwed up as tightly as possible with the press pin and the book surveyed to see that the boards have not slipped and that the book keeps still its even, rounded form.

If the boards have slipped or changed their position in any way, as they are liable to do when pressure is applied, the book must be taken out again and the fault remedied. A little moisture applied to the backing boards will usually prevent their movement.

BACKING. The backing hammer should be taken in the right hand, and with a circular motion, starting from the centre, the sections should be beaten so that they fall one over the other equally on either side. It is very important that each section should lap well over and not be knocked in a zig-zag manner by direct blows, or the leaves inside the book will be creased. The last sections on either side should be well beaten over the boards to ensure a clean sharp groove or joint (*Fig. 54*).

Backing is the most important process in the binding of a book and the most difficult. Rounding and backing are governed by the swell caused in sewing.

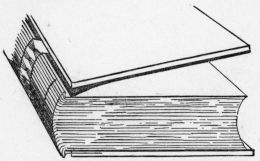

Fig. 55. Method of fixing tapes into 'split boards'

When dealing with a book which has an unusual amount of swell, book and boards should be left projecting 1 in. above the cheeks of the press to prevent the boards slipping. The press should be screwed up and the book slightly backed and then lowered into the right position and the backing finished.

SPLIT BOARDS. A split board is made by pasting a thin and thick board together. For an octavo book an eightpenny mill-board and an 8-oz. strawboard should be cut twice the size of the book, allowing for squares and for trimming the leaves. The thin board should be pasted except in the centre, where a strip of board or paper about 4 in. wide should be laid before pasting. The mill-board is then placed on to the pasted board and nipped in the press.

While this is drying the tapes should be glued on to the waste end-papers, which should then be cut off about $1\frac{1}{2}$ in. from the joint.

The split board is cut down the centre of the unpasted portion, leaving 2 in. splits down the back edge of each board. The boards should be squared to the book with the press and plough or a millboard cutting machine. The split should be opened, the inside of both boards glued, and the strip of end-paper and tapes placed in between, setting the squares and leaving the edge of the board about $\frac{3}{16}$ in. from the back, forming what is called a French joint (*Fig. 55*). A pressing board is placed on either side of the book, level with the back, and the book nipped in the press (*Fig. 56*).

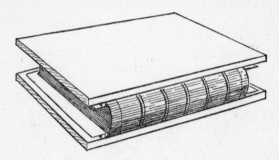

Fig. 56. Book with tins placed inside boards ready to put in press

If the book is to be covered with linen the back must be lined up with a stout piece of cartridge or brown paper cut the exact size of the back, also a piece cut for the hollow. The waste end-paper must be cut in the French joint, about 1 in. on either side at head and tail, to allow the cover to be turned in underneath the back.

The linen is cut for the cover and glued. On the book the squares of the boards are set evenly and at the back $\frac{3}{16}$ in. from the joint. The book is then placed on the glued cover, the hollow placed at the back and the linen drawn over on to the top board (*Fig. 52*). The corners are cut off to mitre and the top and bottom edges of the cover turned in. For this the book stands on the tail over the edge of a pressing board so that the glued edges do not come into contact with the edge of the book. The cover is turned in at the head over the edges of the boards and down between the cuts in the French joint. The book is turned over and the turning-in repeated at the tail. The cover is then turned in at the fore-edges, and the corners mitred.

The cover must be well rubbed down and the folder drawn along the French joint so that the linen sticks to the waste end-papers and tapes between the boards and the back of the book.

HOLLOW BACKS. If a stronger hollow back is required for these bindings in the case of very thick books, it is better to line up the back first with either a strip of leather or calico. A strip of either is cut the size of the back, glued on and well rubbed down.

To make the hollow a piece of cartridge paper is cut a little longer than the back and three times its width; this is folded exactly into three the long way. The back is then glued, and the centre portion of the paper placed on top of the leather or calico and well rubbed down with a folder. The overlapping portion on the right is folded over the back and glued and the left portion brought over and stuck down to this—forming the 'hollow-back'.

The paper projecting beyond head and tail is cut off, and with a sharp penknife inserted into the hollow, each side is cut down about $1\frac{1}{2}$ in. to allow the material used for covering to be turned in.

The end-papers are now pasted and the boards closed on to them. Pressing boards are placed on either side up to the back edges of the boards and the book is put into press. It is left there for a few minutes, taken out and opened, and then put back and left under pressure until dry. This method of pasting down end-papers is called 'pasting down shut'.

CHAPTER X

BOOKS BOUND IN SPLIT BOARDS AND COVERED IN QUARTER- OR HALF-LEATHER WITH LINEN OR PAPER SIDES

The book to be covered in quarter- or half-leather is brought on as in the previous exercise as far as the fixing of the tapes into split boards. When leather is used for covering, the back is not lined up with paper, but the leather is stuck directly on to the back of the book.

The leather back of sheep or niger morocco is cut 1½ in. longer than the back of the book and the width of the back plus 2 in.

Fig. 57. Shoemaker's knife useful for paring edges of leather

This leaves ¾ in. to turn in at head and tail, and 1 in. to come on the boards at either side.

This piece of leather should be carefully pared round the edges to ensure neatness, and a little more should be pared off the head and tail than down the sides.

PARING. For paring, the leather is laid on a smooth marble slab or a litho stone, grain side downwards, and held in position with the left hand, the fingers being on the surface of the leather.

THE PARING KNIFE. For paring the edges only, an ordinary shoemaker's knife serves quite well (*Fig. 57*). It should be sharpened only on the upper side. The side in contact with the leather should be quite flat, but for a slight burr rubbed over in finally setting the knife on the oilstone. When paring, the blade of the knife is laid almost flat upon the edge of the leather and gradually pushed forward by the right hand. According to the angle at which the knife is held the amount of leather removed will vary. The aim is to take off a level shaving of the right thickness and not to leave a series of ridges by uneven cutting (*Fig. 58*). Some

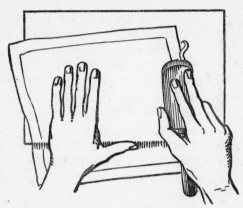

Fig. 58. Paring the edges of the leather cover

practice is required to pare leather, but the neatness of the covering depends largely on even paring. Some leathers will pare better if slightly damped with a sponge and water.

SOAKING. When the strip of niger morocco has been pared it should be slightly damped with a sponge on the grain side, pasted evenly with thick paste on the flesh side, and folded over to soak.

When sufficiently pliable the back should be opened out and laid flat on a clean millboard, pasted surface upward.

The back of the book should be well pasted and the squares adjusted. The book should be held in both hands and the back placed in the middle of the strip of leather. If the book is moved slightly backwards and forwards the leather will adhere to the back. The book is then laid on its side and the leather pulled over equal distances on the two boards. With the folder the leather is rubbed into the French joint on either side.

To turn in the leather at head and tail the book should be taken by the fore-edge and placed upright over the edge of a pressing board with the boards slightly extended. With the hands on each side, pushing back the boards slightly, the leather is folded over into the back by the thumbs, pulling it over the edges of the boards so tightly that no wrinkle or fold is seen.

Fig. 59

SETTING THE HEAD AND TAIL. When the leather has been turned in at the head and tail a piece of string should be tied round in the French joint, and the head and tail set. This is done by moulding the leather with the folder at an angle of 45 degrees from the back to the outer edge, so that it is level with the boards (*Fig. 59*).

The book should now be put in correct shape, and laid over a pressing board with the leather projecting to dry. The leather should not be brought into contact with steel or iron tools while damp, or it will turn black.

When the leather is dry the string is removed, the sides of the book covered with linen or paper, and the end-papers pasted down shut as described in Chapter IX, p. 52.

HALF-BINDING. The same exercise may be extended to half-bindings, using for the corners either vellum tips or larger corners of the same leather as the back.

The corners should be cut out in proportion to the back, the edges pared, stuck on as described for linen corners, but using paste instead of glue.

CHAPTER XI

BOOK SEWN FLEXIBLE, CUT-IN BOARDS, HEAD BANDED AND BOUND IN HALF- OR FULL-LEATHER

A book that is well printed on a good and suitable paper should be selected as worthy of this style of binding.

If the book has already been cased or bound it must be carefully taken to pieces, all weak sections mended, and zig-zag end-papers made as in an earlier exercise. When this has been done, and with end-papers placed on either side, the book should be knocked up quite level at the head and back, placed between two pressing boards also level with the head and back, and put in a lying press, leaving the back of the book about 3 in. above the cheeks of the press (*Fig. 37*). With the press screwed up firmly, the position of the cords should be marked. As these cords form the bands or ridges on the back of the book when it is covered, it is important that they should be placed accurately. The back is marked into six equal portions with a pair of dividers, leaving ½ in. extra at the tail panel. The extra length allowed for this panel is found to be essential for proportion when the book is placed upright on a shelf. With a set-square and pencil heavy lines should be marked across the back at each point, and care should be taken that every section receives a mark.

The book should be taken out of the press, and the end-papers and pressing boards pulled down without displacing the sections. When the book is in the press again slight cuts should be made with a tenon saw about ½ in. from head and tail. These are to allow the kettle stitch to sink level with the back of the book.

The book is now ready for sewing.

SETTING UP THE FRAME FOR SEWING. For flexible sewing the stitching frame described in Chapter VII is required (*Fig. 41*).

Since the book has been marked up for five bands, five lay-cords must be fixed to the crossbar by a simple knot, and five fairly thick cords on to which the book will be sewn set up on the frame in the manner described.

The cords must be moved to correspond with the lines made for them on the back of the book, and must be parallel and perpendicular. When correctly placed they are tightened by the screwing up of the crossbar. A roll of paper or piece of wood kept for the purpose should be pushed in the slot in front of the cords to ensure that they are all in the same plane, and a pressing board placed on the bed of the frame up to the cords for ease in sewing the first section.

CHOICE OF THREAD. Care should be taken in the choice of sewing thread. If the thread is too thick too much swell will be caused. Twenty-five two-cord unbleached bookbinders' linen thread will be found suitable for most books, but if the book consists of many thin sections a thin three-cord silk may be better, as the use of this will reduce the swell.

SEWING FLEXIBLE. The front end-paper is opened where the sheet is inserted, and holes are made with the needle through the pencil marks and into the middle of the inserted sheet. It is then placed face downwards on the stitching frame, head to the right, and holes made to correspond exactly with the cords set up on the frame. Insert the needle with the right hand in the hole made for the kettle stitch at the head; now with the left hand, which is placed in the middle of the section, pass the needle out at the next hole on the left-hand side of the first cord, leaving about 2 in. of thread out at the kettle stitch. Then with the right hand the needle is inserted in the same hole, but at the right-hand side of the first cord—the thread thus making a complete circle round the cord— this being the principle of flexible sewing. The left hand takes the needle again and passes it out at the left-hand side of the next cord and the process is repeated. The remaining cords are treated in the same manner and the thread finally passed out at the tail kettle stitch (*Fig. 43*). The thread must be pulled tight each time it is passed round a cord, but parallel with the sections and not towards you, otherwise the paper may be torn. The next section is now opened in the centre and holes pierced through the pencil marks as before; this is not done by professional sewers, but is a great help to the student, as it ensures all sections being kept quite level at the head, and all stitches being exactly opposite the cords. Place this section face downwards on the already sewn end-paper and insert the needle in the tail kettle stitch. This time it is brought out at the right side of the bottom cord and returned into the same hole on the left side of the cord, the thread being sewn round each cord from tail to head until the head kettle stitch is reached, and when it has been pulled tight is tied to the loose end left in the first section by a double knot. Make the holes in the next section and sew on exactly as first section, but when tail kettle stitch is reached insert the needle between previous two sections, putting needle through the loop formed, and pull thread upwards and parallel with the main cords; this allows the knot to rest in the saw mark (Fig. 39).

Every few sections should be knocked down with a small pressing board, used edgeways between each cord, to avoid undue swell and to keep the sections close together. The last section, which will be the end-paper, when sewn on is fastened off at the kettle stitch with a double knot.

When one needleful of thread is used up another must be tied on (Fig. 40). It is better that it should be joined when the used up thread has completed a kettle stitch, so that the knot can be drawn through the saw mark and rest in the middle of the next section.

When the sewing is completed the cords should be loosened by lowering the bar, the keys removed, and the cord cut off, allowing about 3 in. beyond the book on either side.

Knocking out the swell, glueing-up, rounding and backing, which are the next processes, have already been learned in previous exercises; but the process to follow these differs from that of casing or binding in split boards.

When the book has been backed a pair of millboards are cut to the required size. The size of the book, when the edges have been trimmed, is first calculated and the boards cut about $\frac{1}{4}$ in. larger all round. These are lined on one side with thin paper, nipped in the press to ensure the paper adhering evenly, and stood up to dry. The lining is to counteract the pull of the leather used to cover the book. While the boards are drying the cords of the book may be frayed out.

When dry the lined sides of the boards are placed together and the edges that are to be placed up to the joint or groove of the book are cut with the plough to give a square smooth edge. The

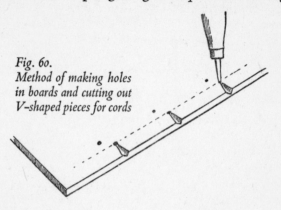

Fig. 60.
Method of making holes
in boards and cutting out
V-shaped pieces for cords

top edges are marked with a set-square to make a perfect right angle with the cut edge, the boards are replaced in the press and cut to the mark made. Two edges of the boards are now cut at right angles, and when squares have been allowed at head, tail and fore-edge, the remaining two sides are marked parallel with the square edges and cut as before. When the pair of boards have been cut they may be tested by reversing one, when any deviation from the truth will be at once apparent.

HOLES FOR LACING-IN. The boards are laid on either side of the book up to the joint and level with the head, if the book has to be cut, and lines are made on them from each cord at right angles to the back up to a line already marked $\frac{3}{8}$ in. from, and parallel to, the back edge of the board (*Fig. 60*). Small V-shaped pieces are cut out on these lines, half the thickness of the board, so that the cords may sink in level with the surface of the board. Holes should be made with a bodkin at the intersections of the lines, and another series made by reversing the boards and making holes about ½ in. away from the first holes towards the tail of the book.

The slips, which have been previously scraped and reduced to silky fibres, are well pasted, and the ends slightly twisted to a point. They are threaded through the first line of holes, and back through the second line made on the reverse side of the board

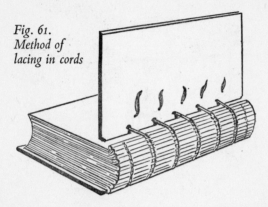

Fig. 61.
Method of
lacing in cords

(*Fig. 61*). When all the slips have been laced in they should be pulled tight, tapped with a hammer to fix them, and cut off close to the board. The knocking-down iron is fixed at the end of the lying press, the board opened and placed on the iron surface, and the slips knocked well down with the hammer. The other side is treated in the same way, care being taken not to bruise the boards, but only to beat the cords level (*Fig. 62*).

THE SHAPE OF THE BOOK. The book should now be examined to see that it is in a good shape, and the joints lightly tapped to the boards. For this the book is placed on the lying press, fore-edge towards the worker. The thumb of the left hand is placed on the front edge of the board, and the joint tapped gently over towards the board. The book is turned over and the process repeated for the other side. During this process the boards must be kept in their proper position, and care must be taken that the book is not twisted.

F

The book is fixed in the lying press, and the back, projecting about 2 in., is coated with thin paste to moisten the glue, which is then removed with a folder or a piece of wood shaped for the purpose. If this surplus glue were left on, the book would not open well. While the back is still moist the cords must be nipped up and straightened with the band nippers.

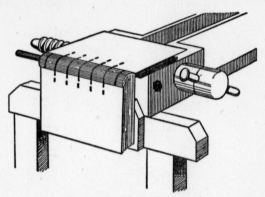

Fig. 62. Knocking down cords

PRESSING. Keeping the book again in perfect shape, tins must be placed on both sides of the boards, level with the joint, and pressing boards outside the tins and level with the back, and the whole put into the standing press, just under the screw to ensure equal pressure (*Fig. 56*). The press is screwed down tightly and left about twelve hours.

CUTTING THE EDGES. When the book has been well pressed it is taken out and the tins removed, and is ready for cutting.

THE KNIFE. It is important, if a smooth edge is to be cut, that the plough knife be ground to a very sharp and smooth edge, the under side kept perfectly flat. The knife should be set accurately in the plough before cutting is commenced, and should just clear both cheeks of the press. The point of the knife can be elevated or lowered by inserting a strip of paper between the knife and the metal plate at the front or back, as is required to correct the position.

The head of the book should first be cut, then the tail, and lastly the fore-edge. When the head is cut, the boards should be placed in their correct positions, and then the front board lowered just the distance required for the square, which is about ⅛ in. for an octavo book. A piece of strawboard is placed between the end-paper and the back board to prevent the knife cutting into that board. The book must be lowered carefully into the cutting press,

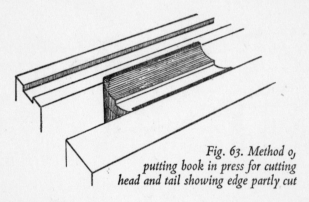

Fig. 63. Method of
putting book in press for cutting
head and tail showing edge partly cut

back towards the worker, until the top edge of the front board is exactly level with the right-hand cheek of the press, and the back board ⅛ in. above and exactly parallel with the left-hand cheek. The press is screwed up tightly with the pin and the cheeks kept parallel as an indication of equal pressure. The plough is placed in position, and the screw turned very gradually each time that the knife is pushed away from the worker.

The tail of the book is cut in the same manner, but this time the back board is lowered a square and the strip of strawboard placed between the front board and the end-paper.

CUTTING THE FORE-EDGE. Before cutting the fore-edge the waste sheet of the end-papers should be cut off flush with the edges of both back and front boards, and marks made on them the width of the square below. These will be the cutting lines. The fore-edge is then made flat by inserting trindles across the back between the book and the boards at the head and tail, to enclose the top and bottom cords (*Fig. 64*). The boards are now at right angles to the book. The back is knocked perfectly flat, and the book is tied with a piece of tape before the trindles are removed, to keep it in position while it is placed in the press.

A cutting board is placed on the left-hand side level with the waste sheet of the end-paper, and one on the right-hand side to

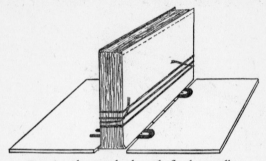

Fig. 64. Showing book made flat by trindles and tied up ready for cutting fore-edge

the mark made as a cutting line. The book and boards should be firmly grasped in the left hand, the trindles removed, and the whole lowered in the press until the right cutting board is just level with the cheek of the press and the left one a square above. The press should be screwed up tightly and the edge cut with the plough (*Fig. 50*).

Before cutting it should be observed that the back is quite flat and the book not twisted in any way, or an uneven cut will result. If the book has been accurately placed and cut the squares of the boards will be equal all round the edges.

CHAPTER XII

EDGE GILDING OR COLOURING, HEAD-BANDING AND LINING-UP

The edges of books are best preserved by gilding. Even if a book has uncut edges the top edge should be cut and gilded or coloured, so that it may be easily dusted. If the book is to be gilded on all three edges the fore-edge is gilded first.

This may be done directly after the edge has been cut and while the book is held flat by the tape, but it must first be taken out of the press to inspect the cutting and replaced with both cutting boards flush with the edge.

SCRAPING THE EDGE. The edge must be scraped perfectly smooth with the rounded edge of a steel scraper, which is held in both hands and moved vigorously away from the worker (*Fig. 65*). It may then be rubbed with a very fine glass paper.

A little Armenian bole or gilders' red chalk, mixed with thin glair into a smooth paste, is rubbed lightly over the edge with a fine sponge or piece of cotton-wool, just sufficient being used to colour the edge. This should be polished with a hard brush. Some gilders mix a little blacklead with the chalk. The object of this is to get a hard, bright surface on which to float the size and to prevent the edge from absorbing the size too readily. Were the gold laid directly on the white paper it would not look so rich when burnished.

When the chalk coating is dry, a sheet of gold must be taken from the book of gold, laid on the cushion and cut into strips a little wider than the edge.

HANDLING GOLD. To handle gold successfully great care is needed. A gold cushion, slightly padded and covered with rough calf, flesh side out, and a gold knife are required (*Figs. 18 and 18A*). The book of gold is laid on the left-hand side of the cushion and opened at the first leaf. The edge of the book is tapped with the gold knife, which causes the leaf of gold to blow half over. The knife is placed near the folded edge of the gold and a light breath will blow the sheet back again over the knife. It may then be lifted out of the book and placed on the cushion, where it is cut to the size required. It is important that both cushion and knife be kept free from grease, or the gold will stick to them and be entirely wasted.

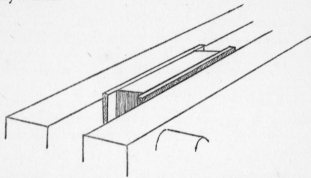

Fig. 65. Book screwed up for scraping and gilding fore-edge

A little bath-brick rubbed on the cushion will free it from grease and enable the gold to be cut cleanly. Before using the knife both sides should be rubbed on the cushion. A cardboard box lid, about 4 in. square, will be found useful to cover up the sheet of gold when not being used.

Edge-gilding size is made by well beating up one white of egg with half a pint of water, leaving it to stand about twelve hours and straining it through fine muslin. Instead, ordinary glair, made from dried albumen as used for leather gilding but diluted with water to about a fourth of its strength, may be used.

SIZING THE EDGE. Before applying the size sufficient gold must be picked up on strips of slightly greased paper with the gold projecting a little beyond the edge. The size should then be applied with a wide camelhair brush and sufficient put on to hold the gold. The strips of gold are laid on to this, the paper being held at each end and drawn away when the gold is released. The edge should be covered with gold in this way.

Care must be taken that there are no lumps or hairs on the edge before the gold is laid on. The edge should now be left to dry. In an ordinary temperature this will take about one hour.

To burnish, a piece of smooth paper, slightly rubbed over with beeswax or slightly greased, should first be laid on to the edge and the bloodstone burnisher passed lightly over. The paper should be held firmly so that no gold is rubbed off. A little beeswax may then be rubbed directly on to the edge with a soft piece of leather and the burnisher applied direct. The burnisher should be held firmly against the shoulder of the worker and moved across the edge to and from the student. Burnishing should be light at first, the pressure increasing each time the edge is gone over until a perfectly bright and solid edge results.

The book is taken from the press and the other edges gilded in the same way. When head and tail are gilded the back of the book must be towards the worker and the scraper used from the back to the fore-edge.

COLOURED EDGES. If, for any reason, the edges of a book are not gilded, they may be left plain or coloured.

Many books during the last century were coloured instead of gilded, lemon colour being largely used. When the colour is evenly put on and well burnished, such edges present a pleasing appearance.

For colouring edges, water dyes are best, but artist's water-colours may also be used if mixed with very thin glair or edge-gilding size.

The book should be screwed up in the lying press as for gilding and the colour applied with a large brush or small sponge. It must be applied very thinly. On the fore-edge the colour should be worked from the centre outwards to either end and taken off quickly to avoid spoiling the other edges. When colouring the head and tail the brush should pass from back to fore-edge.

When dry the coloured edges are greatly improved by burnishing. The book is again screwed up tightly in the press; a little beeswax is rubbed lightly over the edge and the edge polished with a curved agate burnisher.

HEAD-BANDS AND THEIR MAKING. After the decoration of the edge with gold or colour the question of a head-band must be considered.

Two types of head-band are available. One is worked directly on the book. The other is bought by the yard and simply stuck on.

In taking a book from its shelf a pull is exerted on the head-band, so that from a constructional point of view the false head-band is of little use. Apart from this, working the head-band on to the book allows more freedom in choice of silks, which should be selected to harmonize with edges, leather and end-papers.

The head-band gives an ornamental finish to the book, and at the same time has constructional value in preserving the leather at the head and tail and gives a projection similar to that made by the squares of the boards.

A strip of thick vellum, or of leather which has been stiffened with stout paper glued on to it, is cut slightly less than the width of the squares and about $\frac{1}{2}$ in. longer than the width of the back. If it is drawn between the thumb and a folder it will take a slight curve which will fit the round of the back.

The selected silk must be threaded in a fine, long needle, and sufficient must be used to avoid joining. The needle is inserted in the middle of the first section from the inside and brought out just below the kettle stitch on the outside. It is taken over the top of the book, and again inserted in the same hole and out at the back. About two-thirds of the silk should be drawn through. A loop is thus formed, into which the strip of vellum is passed, leaving about $\frac{1}{4}$ in. on the left-hand side. The silk is drawn tightly,

Fig. 66. Making loop into which vellum strip is placed, and the silk drawn tight to hold it

and a pin inserted behind it to hold it in position (*Figs. 66 and 67*). The threaded portion of the silk is now on the outside of the vellum strip and the shorter end in front. The book may be placed in a finishing press or plough, with the fore-edge slightly sloping towards the worker. The threaded end of the silk is brought over the head-band from the back by the right hand and held taut by the left. The other end is taken by the right hand, passed across the needle end and under the vellum, and pulled tight from the back (*Fig. 67*).

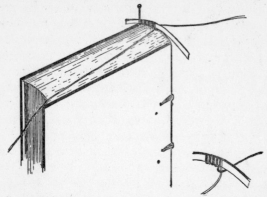

Fig. 67. Method of working head-band and making beading

This, in its turn, is brought over to the front, and the needle end passed across it and under the vellum as before. Care should be taken that the beads formed by these crossings rest at the front of the head-band and touch the edge of the book. When about $\frac{1}{4}$ in. has been worked it should be fastened down to the book by bringing the threaded end of the silk over the vellum from the back and inserting in the middle of a section below the kettle stitch, bringing it out to the back and drawing it tightly. The procedure is then as before, and the tying down takes place at every quarter of an inch.

When the end section is reached the band is fastened down in the same way, but the needle is inserted twice to make a secure finish. The end of silk in front is then passed under the vellum to the back and tied to the threaded end.

When the head- and tail-bands have been worked they must be securely fixed and strengthened by being lined up. The book is placed in the lying press with the back projecting. The head is glued to $\frac{1}{8}$ in. below the kettle stitch and tyings down. This can be done by placing a piece of waste paper across the back and glueing down to it. A piece of brown or cartridge paper is placed

Fig. 68.
Paper stuck
over head bands
to strengthen
them and cover
fastenings

on the glued portion up to the top of the head-band and rubbed down well with a folder. The book is taken out of press, and, with the back of the book resting on the press, the head-band is rubbed down on to the paper from the front, taking care that the head rests in correct position on the leaves of the book. When the glue is dry the paper and vellum ends are cut off close to the silk and the paper torn away from the glued portions, so that no hard edge is left (Fig. 68).

A similar operation takes place at the tail.

CAPPING UP. When the book has been gilded and head-banded, it should be capped up to prevent the edge being damaged in the subsequent processes.

A piece of white paper is cut a little longer than double the size of the book. It is placed up to the joint between the back board and the book, and cut as shown in diagram (Fig. 69). The paper is then folded over head, tail and fore-edge, and secured by pasting slightly the overlapping edges.

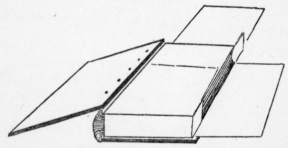

Fig. 69. Method of capping up gilt edges to protect them while covering

It should be folded tightly over the edges, or the squares will not be evident when they are to be set before covering.

CHAPTER XIII

SELECTION OF LEATHER, PARING AND COVERING THE BOOK

The varieties of leather used for bookbinding are described in Chapter III. Small skins are preferable to large ones, as they are usually thinner and more pliable, and require less paring. The use of hard skins should be avoided, since they cause the books in which they are covered to open stiffly. The leather recommended for school work, for half- or full-bound books, is niger morocco. This is usually a pleasing orange red or brown in colour, and is easy to work since it is without much grain.

CUTTING LEATHER TO SIZE. When the leather is selected it must be cut out to size and pared. A piece of paper should be cut the size of the leather required. The book is opened so that the back and both boards lie flat on the paper, and a pencil line drawn round the edges of the board. The book is removed and 1 in. allowed outside this line for turning in. The leather for covering should be cut by this pattern with a knife and straight-edge or shears.

The best part of a skin is down the back. The grain there is close and firm, but becomes soft and loose as it nears the flanks. For school work, however, economy must be studied and, probably, such variations in the leather must be disregarded. Off-cuts, left from cutting out full-bound books, may be used for the backs and corners of half-bound books. Slight unevenness of colour need not be deemed a defect. To obtain an equal dyed surface the skin is subjected to a bath of acid, which tends to injure its wearing qualities.

In ordering leather for small work it is as well to ask for it to be shaved to a medium thickness. This will save time in paring.

When the leather has been cut, the book should be opened and laid upon it, and a pencil mark made round the boards, on the flesh or underside of the leather. This will show where the back and boards come and will be a guide for paring (*Fig. 70*).

PARING. A smooth marble slab, 1 in. thick and about 1 ft. square, is required for this process, with a French paring knife slightly rounded on the cutting edge (*Fig. 11*). A piece of leather pasted round the bottom of the blade will make this more convenient to hold. In sharpening such a knife it must be ground only

Fig. 70. Book laid on leather cover and marked round for paring. When leather had been pared and pasted, the book is laid on in position and leather pulled over as Fig. 72

on its upper side with a gradually tapering edge, and kept perfectly flat on the underside, like a chisel. After being ground it must be finished to a smooth keen edge on the oil-stone. A very slight burr is obtained on the underside by rubbing on the paring stone. This is needed to give a little bite when the knife is used perfectly flat.

The cover is held in position on the paring stone with the left hand, the fingers on the top and the thumb holding the leather on the edge of the stone (*Fig. 58*). The paring should be done away from the worker and directly over the thumb.

The amount of paring necessary will depend on the thickness and nature of the leather. For an ordinary cover it will only be necessary to pare from just within the marks made for the turning in, and down the back, a little wider than the book, to allow the boards to open freely in the joints. The head and tail of the back must be pared especially thin to allow for the double thickness of leather when it is turned in on the back. Paring should start just inside the marks made, and should be so gradual that no ridge is formed.

When the paring is finished the cover should be laid on the stone and the fingers should be run over the leather to test its smoothness. Any inequalities will show when the book is covered.

Paring is a difficult process, and it is most probable that in early attempts the student will cut through the leather.

CUTS IN LEATHER. Cuts may be joined up when the book is in process of covering, if they are not too large and if they do not come across the joints. When the cover is being pared the stone must be kept perfectly clean and clear of bits of leather. If shavings get under the leather the passage of the knife over the surface is checked, and a cut is found to result.

BANDS. The capping up of the book has been described in Chapter XII. It must now be examined carefully to discover if the bands are quite true. If they are not, they should be again nipped up with the band-nippers and straightened.

CUTTING CORNERS. The back corners of each board should be cut off with a sharp knife. For an octavo book ⅛ in. will be sufficient. The boards should be thrown back and the corners cut off with a cut sloping slightly from the inside (*Fig. 71*). More freedom is thus given to the joint when the leather is turned in and the book is able to be tied up when covered, to ensure a neater head cap.

*Fig. 71.
Back corners
of boards cut
off before
covering for
tying up*

The cover is now well pasted with a thick paste applied with a brush. Several applications should be made to distribute the paste evenly, and lumps or hairs should be removed. The cover is folded in two with the pasted side inside, and is left to soak for a few minutes to make it more pliable in working.

While the leather is soaking, a little paste is put under and on the top of the slips, and the back of the book is well pasted. Care must be taken not to get paste under the head-bands at head and tail.

COVERING. The cover is opened, and laid, pasted side up, on a clean straw- or millboard, the fingers being rubbed over it to smooth down the paste. The squares of both boards are set at the head and tail, and the closed book is laid, fore-edge towards the worker, on to the cover, allowing the inch on all sides for turning in (*Fig. 70*). The remaining leather is drawn over the back and on to the other side, and is pulled slightly towards the fore-edge.

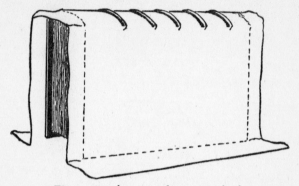

Fig. 72. Leather cover drawn over book

The book stands on its fore-edge on a piece of waste paper, and the back is slightly moistened with a sponge, and the leather made to stick on either side of the bands by nipping with the band nippers (*Figs. 72 and 73*). This causes the leather to pucker slightly in the joints. The waste paper is removed, and the book laid again on the covering board, with the fore-edge towards the worker. The leather is lifted from each side in turn, smoothed down, and rubbed slightly from back to fore-edge with the palm of the hand. It should then lie perfectly flat on the boards, and be in contact with the back between the bands.

The leather is turned in at the fore-edges by placing the left hand between the book and lower board and pressing the leather down with the folder square over the edges of the board. To turn in at the head, the book is placed on the paring stone or covering board so that the boards and back are flat with the head projecting slightly over the edge. A little paste is put on the outside of the leather that will turn in under the head-band. The book is supported on the left arm and the boards pressed down away from the head-band. The leather is turned in under the head-band and over the edges of the boards, care being taken that no paste gets on the head-band. A folder is used to smooth down the leather round the edges of the boards, and at the head-band where it has

Fig. 73. Method of using bandnippers for nipping up
the bands in covering

been pared thin it must be squeezed together, sufficient being left out to turn over and cover the top of the head-band, to form a head cap. No rucks must be left in the leather under the head-band, or the back will be unsightly. The tail is turned-in in the same manner (*Fig. 74*).

The leather at the corners of the boards should be pulled over as far as possible and made to meet at an angle of 45 degrees. The folds are then cut off with scissors about ¼ in. above the board and one edge lapped over the other, moulding the leather over the extreme corners as neatly as possible (*Fig. 75*). The squares must be looked at and corrected if they have been moved during the covering.

HINGES. To obtain a good hinge, each board should be opened in turn and placed square with the joint. For this, which is perhaps the most important part of covering, a folder or straight-edge is placed up to the joint. The board is held in the left hand and pushed so that the edge is parallel with and close up to the

Fig. 74. *Method of turning-in leather*

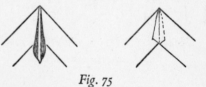

Fig. 75

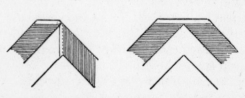

Fig. 76. *Two ways of mitreing corners*

top of the joint (*Fig. 77*). The board is closed well into the joint and must not be opened again till the leather is dry. A piece of thin thread is tied tightly along the joints and over the head and tail into the back, where the corners of the boards have been cut away. This enables the head and tail caps to be set easily and neatly.

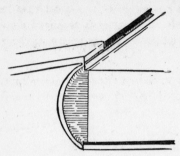

Fig. 77. After turning-in the leather, the boards must be pushed well over the joint

HEAD AND TAIL CAPS. The book is held in the left hand, the tail resting over a folder or backing board, so that the tail cap is not crushed. The leather is pressed into the corners of the head cap between the head-band and the thread, and the projecting leather is tapped over the head-band. The book is turned over to rest the cap on the board, and the back is rubbed with the folder to make a neat and firm edge. Tail caps are treated in the same way (*Fig. 78*).

The book should now be held firmly in the left hand with its fore-edge resting on the bench, and the bands should be nipped up again with nickel band nippers, to make them straight and to make the leather stick on either side. Each panel between the bands should be pressed down with a band stick or folder (*Fig. 73*).

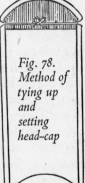

Fig. 78. Method of tying up and setting head-cap

When the covering is complete the book should be sponged over with clean water, stood squarely on its fore-edge for a few minutes, and then placed between clean papers on either side and left under a slight weight till dry. This will take about twelve hours. Care must be taken that the leather, while damp, does not come

G

into contact with any iron or steel tools, or a black stain will result which will be almost impossible to remove.

All operations in covering require great care and accuracy to ensure success. Tools and materials required should be at hand before the work is commenced, as many of the processes allow of no delay.

OPENING BOARDS. When the cover is well set, but not absolutely dry, the boards should be opened. Each board in turn should be taken in the left hand and opened. At the same time it should be pressed towards the joint, in which a folder is placed with the right hand. The board and joint should thus be pushed together so that the boards open just on the top of the joint, as in Fig. 77. If, for any reason, the boards open stiffly, or are inclined to come away from the joint, the leather should be damped slightly and the board gently tapped with the hammer into its correct position.

MITREING CORNERS. Corners are sometimes mitred during the covering. This is the method generally used by craftsmen. When the cover has been drawn over and the bands nipped up, before the fore-edge is turned in the corners of the leather are cut off at an angle of 45 degrees, allowing the thickness of the board beyond the corner. For this the knife (*Fig. 57*) should be very sharp. The book should be laid on a paring stone, the knife placed underneath the board, and the projecting leather at the corner pared away. It must not be cut off too bluntly, or the overlap will project, yet, if too much is pared away the mitre will be imperfect. When turned in the overlapping edges should just meet at an angle of 45 degrees. For this method of mitreing, the leather at the head and tail is turned in first and the fore-edge afterwards. In bringing the leather over it should be moulded neatly and squarely at the corners (*Fig. 76*).

If the corners are not mitred in covering the process must take place after the boards have been opened. The book is placed with the front board open on pressing boards or on another book, so that it lies flat. A large pressing board should be underneath, and the whole can then be turned round without fear of marking the leather on the underside of the cover.

With a pair of dividers, lines are marked to show the margin of leather required. A cut is made along each line with a knife and straight-edge, taking care that the cuts meet exactly at the corners. The surplus leather cut off is then removed. To mitre the corners, a slanting cut is made through the overlapping leathers from the corner of the boards to the corner of the leather margin. This should be at an angle of 45 degrees. The leather is well damped and lifted, the overlapping pieces removed, the leather pasted, and the two edges neatly joined together. If the

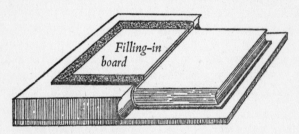

*Fig. 79. Book in position for tooling inside border
and for filling-in*

leather is thick it will sometimes need paring at the extreme corners to ensure neatness. It should be well tapped down and rubbed smooth with the folder (*Fig. 75*).

FILLING-IN. When the four corners are mitred, a piece of thick cartridge paper or thin sheet board should be cut to fill-in the board up to the margin of the leather. The paper or board chosen for filling-in should be slightly larger than double the size required for both boards. A straight edge is cut on the longest side and the paper is folded in two by the cut edge, giving a perfect right angle. The fold is cut off by a line perfectly parallel with its edge. The right angle of the filling-in board is fitted into the left-hand top corner of the turned-in leather. A finger of the right hand should be rubbed on top of the board, just over the back edge of the board of the book. This will make a mark on the filling-in, by which it can be cut. With a knife point a mark should be made on each side of the filling-in board where it fits up to the right-hand side of the turn-in, and a cut made through these marks.

PRESSING. The other filling-in board or paper should be cut in the same manner for the other side of the book. Both pieces should be well pasted, placed in position and rubbed down. If they are at all thick, tins should be placed inside each board, and the book, with a pad of paper on either side up to the edge of the back, should be given a nip in the press. Care must be taken in placing tins inside. The tin should be placed on to the board just up to its back edge, and then tin and board closed together. If the tin is placed on the book and the board closed on to it, it is apt to lever the filling-in board away from the back edge.

The book may be allowed to dry in the press or may be taken out and the boards left open to dry.

The object of filling-in up to the leather on the inside of the boards is not only to equalize the thickness there, but also to make the boards lie flat to the book, since the contraction caused in the drying counteracts the pull of the leather outside.

When the book is dry it is ready for 'finishing'. Before commencing the tooling, however, it should be carefully opened—by taking a few leaves at a time from the beginning of the book and pressing them gently down in the centre of the fold, going right through the book. Then turn the book round and commence from the end, and open in the same way. This will ensure the book opening well and prevent the back being broken, which might happen if the book were opened in the middle first. This especially applies to 'flexible' sewn books.

CHAPTER XIV

DESIGNING AND FINISHING

The process involved in lettering the title and in the decoration of the book by stamps in either blind or gold tooling is termed 'finishing'. Before giving details of this, suggestions may be useful for the designing of book covers when hand tools are employed.

LETTERS. All books should be lettered, whether decorated or not. The sets of type or hand letters illustrated in most toolcutters' catalogues are unsuitable for school use, being poor in design and often not easily legible. Fancy or eccentric types should be avoided, and three or four sizes of a good Roman letter should be chosen. A better plan is to have the letters specially cut, though this naturally entails greater expense. Illustration of a good Roman letter is in Fig. 80, together with a sans-serif letter of a type frequently used on modern bindings.

FILLET. Another essential tool is the fillet, a brass or gunmetal wheel, with its edge cut to the thickness of the line required. It is used for making long straight lines. The fillet is usually about $3\frac{1}{2}$ in. in diameter, with 1 in. filed out so that the line may be begun and finished at given points as in mitreing (*Fig. 20, p. 15*).

LINES. For making shorter lines a set of line pallets is needed. These are required for tooling mitred panels on the backs of books or for short lines needed in making patterns for the sides (*Fig. 81*), and might be made by the students themselves.

GOUGES are used for curved lines. They are made in sets of ten to twelve arcs of a circle. A set of flat short gouges is useful (*Fig. 81 and Fig. 21, p. 15*).

To make the longer line, pallets and gouges $\frac{1}{8}$ in. sheet brass may be used. It is sawn down roughly to shape, filed to the thickness required on the surface, and the other end filed to a point to

A B C D
A B C D

Fig. 80

fit in a wooden handle. Long gouges may be beaten to the curve required on a steel rod or other curved surface.

Shorter lines and gouges may be made from brass rods heated and beaten out flat or curved and filed to shape.

Set of line pallets *Round Gouges* *Flat Gouges*

Fig. 81

DOTS. Three or four sizes of 'dot' will be required. These may be made by the student from brass rods filed round for some distance from the point so that sight of the end of the tool may be obtained when working.

RINGS. Two or three rings will also be required (*Fig. 82*), which may also be made from brass rods. A hole is drilled first in the centre and then the brass filed away as for the dot, but leaving a thin line round the centre. If the first attempt is unsuccessful the surface may be rubbed down on fine emery board, the hole drilled a little deeper and the filing done again. When completed the ring must be a perfect circle and even in thickness.

LEAVES. Leaves of different sizes and shapes may be cut and filed from brass rods, the veins being cut out with a graver. The simpler the form of these the better (*Fig. 82*).

Fig. 82. A few suggestions for tools

When making such tools as these a small vice will be found necessary to hold the rods being filed, and the files used must be fine.

OTHER SIMPLE TOOLS. Other simple units will suggest themselves to combine with lines and dots in making patterns. Three sizes of square (*Fig. 82*) will be easily filed, and such units as those following will be useful in designing corners.

A flower or two added to these units will enable the student to invent simple but effective designs.

If tool cutting is beyond the capability of the student, a variety of tools can be obtained ready cut. No tools for hand tooling should be larger than ½ in. square, or they will be found difficult to impress successfully.

PRINCIPLES OF DESIGN. A few principles may be laid down to govern the student in designing for book covers.

Decoration of a book cover should be in harmony with the nature of the work. The design ought always to be simple and flat without shading.

The decoration of the flat surface of a book cover should, generally speaking, be purely ornamantal and not pictorial.

Tools used in the design should be elemental in form, without any eccentricity, so that they will bear orderly repetition without becoming monotonous. They should be grouped or distributed, according to some geometrical plan, within a well-defined border.

All pattern must be harmonious in its detail and sympathetic in the nature of its development.

The lettering should always be considered as part of the scheme of decoration, and should be in character and proportion an integral part of the design. If used on the sides it may be massed in the centre or made a decoration in the border, but in either case it must be set out as part of the design, and not, as often appears, added as an afterthought (see Plates IV and VI).

Should the book suggest symbolic treatment a lapse into pictorial treatment should be avoided. An endeavour must be made to express in as direct a manner as possible the chief characteristics of the book.

The student should aim at making use of construction for decorative purposes. Decoration begins with the sewing of the book and should be felt or considered in all subsequent processes.

Lastly, a simple, well-spaced design, having regard to the worth of the material, has a much more dignified and restful beauty than any amount of indiscriminate gold tooling can possess.

LETTERING is the most important feature of the decoration. All books should be lettered on the back. If they are not thick enough for the lettering to go across they may be lettered up the back from tail to head.

In the workshop lettering is often carried out with brass type screwed up into a type holder. This is a quick method when many volumes of the same title are to be lettered, but hand letters are advocated for school use, as they are more practicable and allow greater freedom of arrangement.

In setting out the lettering for the back of a book the words should first be written out in lines. If the title of the book is to be 'Bookbinding as it should be taught in schools', this should be roughly written out in four lines, and the number of letters in each line counted, taking the space between each word as a letter.

A strip of tough but thin paper the height of the panel to be lettered and about 4 in. long should be cut. In the middle of this the width of the back should be marked and a fold made exactly in the centre.

The lettering is arranged in four lines, and the size of letter which will be most suitable must be selected. The letter B should be impressed four times as in Fig. 83, leaving a little more space top and bottom of the panel than between each line.

With the dividers the distance from the top of each letter should be marked and a fine pencil line drawn through these points. The centre letter is now impressed just under the top pencil line and the other letters worked on either side as in Fig. 83. Each line is treated in the same way.

Lettering looks best arranged in equal lines and spaced out so that it conveniently fills the panel.

11	BOOKBINDING	B
12	AS IT SHOULD	B
9	BE TAUGHT	B
10	IN SCHOOLS	B

Fig. 83. *Marking out paper for hand lettering on back of book*

Judgement in spacing is needed with such different widths of letter as in M, W, I and J, and the letters must be worked in to accommodate each other on either side of the centre.

IMPRESSING THE LETTERS. When the letters are impressed they should be held firmly in the right hand with the thumb on

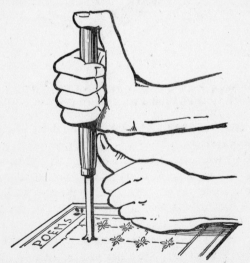

Fig. 84. *Method of holding and guiding tool*

the top of the handle and guided into their positions with the thumb of the left hand (*Fig. 84*). The upper side of the letter is usually filed with a nick so that the right way up may be readily seen.

LETTERING THE BOOK. When the lettering has been correctly impressed the paper should be attached to the book in correct position. The top panel but one is the usual place if the book has been sewn on five bands. If the book is linen-covered it is lettered usually on the back towards the head. The book is placed in a finishing press, with a piece of paper on either side and with the back projecting about 3 in. It should be screwed up tightly. The ends of the strip of paper on which the lettering is impressed are pasted and placed in correct position on the book with the pasted edges brought down on to the paper on each side of the book so that it is held firmly while the impressions are made through the paper on to the back with the heated letters (*Fig. 85*).

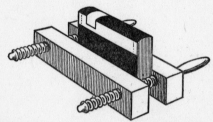

Fig. 85. Method of working lettering on back through paper pattern. Note paper strip round boards to stick pattern to

HEATING THE LETTERS. The letters should be placed round the stove in order, from right to left, and heated just so much that they stop hissing when cooled on a wet piece of cotton wool.

Each letter should be held upright and pressed slightly from side to side and from top to bottom. It is possible to follow the outline of the tool in this way so that all parts of the letter are impressed with equal clearness.

Should the same title be worked on the side of the book it might be preferable to use two lines instead of four. It should be marked out on paper as before, but arranged to form two equal lines by giving a little more space between the letters in the second line.

This lettering paper must also be fixed firmly to the book. To do this a strip of paper should be attached to the top edge of the lettering paper, taken under the board of the book, brought again to the front and pasted to the bottom edge of the lettering paper (*Fig. 86*).

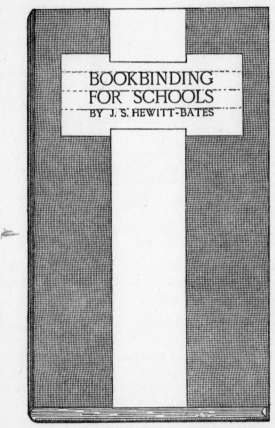

Fig. 86. Method of attaching lettering paper to side of linen book to get 'blind' impression

Lettering on the side of a book looks well if placed towards the top. It should in any case be higher than the centre. If it is to be worked as a decoration in the border—a pleasing and interesting method of introducing lettering—it must be worked out with the design.

When the lettering has been impressed with warm letters the paper should be removed. It will be found that some papers leave a thin coating of fibre on the impressions. This can be removed from a leather-covered book with a damp sponge. If the book is covered in linen the fibre must be taken off carefully with the point of the dividers moistened with the tongue. Thin bank paper is best, as it is not liable to stick under the heat.

A BLIND IMPRESSION. The paper removed, each letter should be impressed again to ensure evenness and straightness, making what is called a blind impression. If the book is to have no other tooling it may be prepared to receive the gold.

For a linen-covered book it is only necessary to paint in the impressions with glair. A fine sable brush is best for this. If too much glair is applied so that it spreads beyond the impressions, a dirty appearance will be given to the lettering round the gold.

Glair is made by beating up the white of one egg with about half that quantity of vinegar. It should be well beaten up so that it goes into a hard froth, allowed to stand for a day and then strained off. A little powdered camphor added will preserve the glair and make it non-odorous.

Dried albumen may be bought. When sufficient water has been added to make it about the thickness of milk, and the crystals dissolved, it must be strained and is then ready for use.

PREPARATION OF LEATHERS. Leathers need some prepara-tion before glairing-in. Calf and sheep, which are very porous, need washing over with paste water. A little ordinary flour paste put on a wet sponge must be rubbed well all over the leather to fill up the pores, and this must be allowed to dry before the glairing is done.

Some niger moroccos are slightly porous and need paste wash-ing. Levant moroccos are less porous, and need only be washed over with vinegar before the glairing-in.

To get the best results in tooling the glair should not be too dry. If the glair is too thick there is a tendency for it to cake on the surface of the leather or turn white; if this should be so it is better washed off and the pencilling done again. A clear and bright appearance on the surface of the leather shows that the glair is in good condition for working.

The letters are placed round the stove as before to be heated while the gold is laid on. A sheet of gold is taken from the gold book, laid on the cushion and cut into strips wide enough to cover the lettering. A little vaseline is put on a small piece of cotton wool and rubbed on the back of the hand to distribute it evenly, making what is called a 'grease cotton'.

A larger piece of cotton wool formed into a flat pad by pressure on a flat surface or the back of the hand makes a pad to lay on the gold. When this is slightly greased by rubbing across the hair or the greased hand of the worker the gold will adhere to it and may be picked up from the cushion.

LAYING ON THE GOLD. The blind impression of the lettering should be greased over evenly with the vaseline in the grease cotton to hold the gold down. The gold is picked up with the laying-on pad and pressed over the letters. If it breaks in the impressions another piece of gold must be laid on. To make the second layer adhere the worker should breathe lightly on the first layer of gold.

The gold should be pressed firmly in the impression so that the position for the letters may be seen easily.

The first letter is taken from the stove, held on the cooling pad until it ceases to hiss, and is pressed firmly in the impression already made. The letter should be rocked from side to side in the manner already described, but care must be taken not to hesitate with the tool or move it off the impression, or the result will be blurred. It is also essential to have the surface of the tool clean and bright. It should be rubbed lightly on a piece of suède calf after cooling. The flesh side of any leather would do for this and would free the tool from steam or moisture.

'Putting down' letters or tools requires practice before a good result can be obtained, but if these directions have been carefully followed the student should, with perseverance, get satisfactory results.

CLEANING OFF GOLD. When all letters have been put down the surplus gold is rubbed off with a gold rubber. This may be bought from a supplier of bookbinders' materials or made by cutting pure bottle rubber into fine strips, putting the strips into a jar to soak in paraffin oil for a day, and then working the rubber up into a lump convenient to use.

After the gold has been cleaned off the surface should be rubbed over with benzine applied with a small piece of cotton wool. This removes the grease used for laying on the gold. Any letters which are not solid should be glaired-in again. When dry the gold can be laid on and the letter put on a second time.

It is found sometimes that the gold does not adhere properly. In this case the tool has not been hot enough, the glair has been too dry or the pressure uneven or insufficient. If the tools have been the right heat and the impression even and firm, the letters should be clear and bright. Tools that are too hot give the gold a scorched appearance, as they burn the surface of the leather.

If faulty tooling causes gold to stick beyond the impressions that cannot be removed by the rubber or benzine, this should be picked out with the moistened point of dividers.

CHAPTER XV

MAKING PATTERNS
FOR BLIND OR GOLD TOOLING

With the few simple tools illustrated (*Figs. 81 and 82*) numerous patterns can be made for the tooling of book backs and sides.

DESIGNING PANEL FOR BACK. In designing a panel for a leather-covered book, the size of the panel must be marked accurately on a piece of paper. For the purposes of the design it may be assumed that the book is a crown octavo (7½ in. by 5 in.) (*Fig. 87*).

The measurements of the depth of the panel and the width should be marked on a strip of paper and a line drawn round. This will form the outside line of the panel, and if only a one-line mitred panel is desired this is all that is needed as a guide. It may be stuck on each panel as was done for lettering, and the lines worked through the paper to give a blind impression.

The second panel is always reserved for lettering.

When dots are worked in as in panel 3 (*Fig. 87*), these are put in through the paper, and panel 4 would be worked the same way, the flower being put in the centre. Panel 5 would be worked by drawing in the inner line and making an angle of 45 degrees at the corners on which the leaves would be worked.

In making the paper patterns for No. 6 the three leaves would be placed in each corner as for No. 5, the paper folded down the centre and the gouges stamped in, while the paper is folded so that they will be symmetrical. When the paper is opened and the flower put in, the panel is complete.

Only one style of pattern is chosen and repeated for each panel.

When the paper pattern has been made out successfully it must be placed in correct position on each panel so that the outside lines of all the panels are in alignment. Each end of the paper

pattern should be pasted and stuck to the paper on the sides of
the book. Blind impressions are then made through the paper, as
was described for the lettering (*Fig. 85*).

Should the book be in a full leather binding a design must be
made for the sides and for the inside where the leather is turned
down to the end-papers.

Patterns for this inside margin may be made with the tools
which were used on the back. A pattern such as
is shown in Fig. 88 would be appropriate. For a
single line design such as this it will not be necessary to make a paper pattern, but the tools may
be worked directly. The board of the book is
opened and placed on a pressing board or wooden
block to be perfectly flat (*Fig. 79*).

MARKING THE LINES. The lines are marked as
on the sketch with dividers, which are guided
round the edge of the board, having one leg or
point outside the edge, the other marking the position of the line. The outer line is marked quite near
the edge to be seen when the book is closed, the
inner one is made where the end-paper will come,
and a third is marked in between. These lines
should then be blinded in more firmly with a
warm piece of line guided by a straight-edge.
The three leaves are stamped in with warm tools.
If they are placed down very lightly at first they
may be corrected should their position not be
exactly true. Dots and rings may then be put on
in the same manner and the whole repeated on
the inside of the other cover.

DESIGNING THE SIDES. A design should now
be prepared for the outside of the cover. If lines
are to be drawn round the side these will be
marked round with dividers, except at the back
edge of the board, where the line must be marked
with a straight-edge.

Fig. 87.

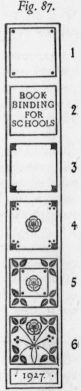

Tools used

Fig. 88

If a more complicated design is desired a paper pattern must be made out. The outside line is marked on the cover with dividers and a paper cut to fit exactly within the lines. This gives the space the design is to occupy. If the design is to be confined to the corners one corner only need be worked out. Still using the tools which were employed to design the back, a simple pattern such as that in Fig. 89 could be worked out. The straight lines will first be drawn. In the corners faint diagonals will guide the position of the tools. If the tools are held in the flame of a candle they will make a black impression on the paper. The flower will be put on first at the top corner, then the leaf on the diagonal line on either side; the other two leaves will be added on either side of the first, the gouges put in to join up the leaves, and a bit of straight line forms the stalk of the flower.

When worked out the paper pattern should be attached in the correct position in each corner by tipping the corners with paste. The lines are indicated at the corners and each corner in turn worked through the paper with warm tools.

When the paper is removed the corners should be moistened with the tip of the finger and lifted carefully while damp. This will prevent the surface of the leather from being damaged.

When the four corners are worked and the paper removed the lines should be joined up with a piece of line abut 1 in. long run along the side of a straight-edge.

Fig. 89

FILLING IN CENTRE PANEL. Should the student wish to fill in the centre panel in this early exercise the design would be most successful if based on a diaper.

A line might be marked about ¼ in. within the inner line of the border on the book and a paper cut to fit this. The paper can be folded from side to side and from head to tail to fix the centre lines each way. If the paper is

H

Fig. 90. Two methods of working diaper patterns

then folded exactly into four each way points will be obtained where lines should meet in the diapers (*Fig. 90*).

The tools are worked in each space or distributed where the lines cross in each diaper (see Plate VII and Fig. 90). The lines might be a feature of the design.

If a more elaborate pattern is desired the paper should be folded in the centre each way, dividing it into four parts. One quarter of the pattern should be sketched in pencil and gouges chosen to fit the lines. When one corner has been designed the paper should be folded over and the tools worked through. The half thus designed may be worked through the paper again, giving the complete pattern (see Plate IV).

When the student has become familiar with diapers other designs may be made in a similar manner. A repeat of simple tools forms a border based on squares (see Plate V and Fig. 93. Figs. 91 and 92 are suggestions for back panels).

Fig. 91   Fig. 92

Such designs as these should show evidence of arising naturally from the use of tools rather than the pencil. In some cases the pattern may be divided into squares, and the working will be facilitated if the designs are worked on squared paper (about ten squares to the inch). This saves time in measuring out.

Constructional parts of a binding lend themselves for decorative purposes. In bindings such as those shown in the Frontispiece and Plate V, the design springs from the bands on which the

*Fig. 93. A paper pattern worked from impressions of tools
cut by students*

book was sewn, and may possess the additional merit of being peculiarly applicable to the book.

When a design is constructed in this manner, the paper pattern must be measured for the panel as before and folded across the centre each way. The point of a compass should be placed in the centre and a circle drawn round just to touch the outer gouge lines. A corner may then be sketched in. If this is folded over from right to left and rubbed down the lines will be transferred to the other quarter. When folded again the whole design may be produced.

The design for the side of the book may be worked in the same way, but the lower panels are left a little longer to match the panel on the back and the upper panels may be left empty for lettering.

Any patterns made out on paper must be stuck on in position and worked through on to the book with warm tools, after which they may be tooled in gold or blind. Should blind tooling be desired the leather must be slightly damped and the tools worked in again. They must be heated only slightly or, the leather being moist, they will be burnt in. Metal straight-edges must not come into contact with the leather while it is damp, or it will be stained. A boxwood ruler should be used if needed for working-in the lines.

The tools must be worked in again and again until the impression is a dark even colour, and when the leather is dry a final impression is made to brighten the design. Gold and blind tooling look well together if designed with that idea in view.

When preparing for gold tooling the paper through which the design has been worked must be carefully removed, and any tools that have not made a clear impression worked again, since in the subsequent washing the impressions of the tools are apt to dry out.

The preparation needed depends on the nature of the leather. Calf and sheep skins must be rubbed with paste on a clean sponge to fill up the pores. A wash over with vinegar is usually sufficient for goat or morocco. When this is dry the impressions of the tools must be painted in with glair. When this is dry the gold is laid on and the pattern tooled. In classes where only a few hours each week are devoted to the subject it is important to prepare and glair only what can be tooled in the time allotted. If left the preparation will be too dry and must be washed off again.

TOOLING. In tooling a full-bound leather book this procedure is followed. The inside margins are tooled first, and this portion is prepared separately. If the book is bound in morocco both inside margins should be washed with vinegar, and the book should stand up with its boards open to dry. When dry the impressions are glaired-in, and for successful tooling the glair must not be allowed to dry so much that it turns white or cakes on the surface. It must not be put on the leather until the vinegar is dry, or it will soak in and have little power to make the gold stick.

USE OF FILLET. The tools should be selected and placed on the stove. A line fillet for working the lines, a leaf, a circle and dot will be required. While these are being heated the gold may be laid on. The book should be placed with one board open over pressing boards or finishing block to make it firm for working (*Fig. 79, p. 83*). The gold is cut into strips slightly wider than the margin to be tooled, which is greased with vaseline on a piece of cotton wool. The gold is laid on with the cotton wool pad in the manner described in Chapter XIV, p. 93, pressed well into the impression, but not rubbed. Gold should be laid on all round the margin. The book should then be placed with the fore-edge towards the worker. The fillet is cooled till it stops hissing. It is then taken by the bottom of the handle, in the right hand; and, with the top resting on the worker's shoulder, is guided in the impression by the left-hand thumbnail into the inner line on the right-hand side margin, which is the nearest line to the left hand. With a firm pressure on the fillet it is run along the line (*Fig. 94*). It should be lifted when about ½ in. from the corner, and the wheel turned back with the nail of the

Fig. 94. Method of using fillet when mitreing

left thumb so that the point can be put down to finish the line at the mitre. It should not be pushed too far forward so that the point is dug in. The other two lines are put in in the same way, the book is turned round, and the lines on the fore-edge margin put in. In doing this the starting point must be adjusted so that the point will join up at the mitre of the lines already put in. The book should be turned again and the remaining lines put in. The leaves are then put in the corners. This tool should be held with the thumb on top of the handle and placed in each impression with a slight rocking motion (*Fig. 84, p. 89*). A leaf should always be held so that it works from point to stalk, and the book should be turned to fit this position. The rings and dots are then put in round the border, remembering that the smaller the surface of the tool the less pressure it requires. When all the pattern has been tooled the surplus gold should be rubbed off with the gold rubber.

A few important points should be observed by the student when working lines with a fillet. A good light is very important, and the best view of the blind impression is usually obtained with the light coming from the left or across the lines.

Should the fillet be too hot, it is cooled by revolving in a basin of cold water, but it must be freed from moisture before being used. When cooled the edge should be cleaned on a pad.

When working it is important that the fillet should be guided into its place with the left thumbnail. The importance of this cannot be overestimated, for in this way the fillet is steadied and enabled to be placed on the impression without difficulty.

When ending a line the fillet should be held back so that the point does not dig into the leather, but in running the line straightness will be obtained by holding the fillet as upright as possible.

The fillet should run smoothly, or it will slide along the line instead of revolving and will remove the gold. A little olive oil put on the axle occasionally will facilitate this.

In working with the other tools the pressure applied should vary according to the size of the tool. Lines, dots, and small gouges need very little pressure. Gouges should always be sighted from the inside of the curve and should be put down firmly without sliding, but with a slight rocking motion. All tools are cut with slightly rounded surfaces so that this motion can be given without digging in the edges. In working the tools on the sides a tin placed under the board will make it firmer for tooling, or a small book might be placed in the finishing press with boards open as shown in Fig. 95.

When striking the flower or similar tools the face of the tool should be held about ¼ in. above the blind impression and in the

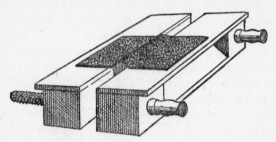

Fig. 95. Book in finishing press ready for tooling sides

same position, and a sight of the impression obtained. It should then be quickly lowered and struck, pressing in the centre first, and then slightly rocking from side to side, but without moving it from the impression. The length of time the tool should be held down varies with its size and the condition of the preparation.

The best results in tooling are obtained by using the tool as cool as possible to make the gold adhere and by a firm and decided pressure. It is only by experience and much practice that the correct heat and pressure can be judged. If, after rubbing off, it is seen that the gold has failed to stick in a few places, these must be reglaired, and, when dry, more gold should be laid on and retooled.

Finally, it is the author's belief and maxim, that the happier the worker is, the brighter the gold will be. Pleasure in the work itself and confidence in the result are the greatest assets to success.

INLAYING. When the student has become proficient in blind and gold tooling, more advanced decorative exercises may be attempted. Pleasing effects are obtained by tooling dots, leaves, and flowers over inlays of various colours.

Leather for inlaying must be pared so thin that there is left only the colour on the bark side. In doing this the leather is cut into strips, damping thoroughly on both sides with a sponge, and pared on the paring stone with a shoemaker's knife (*Fig. 57*). The knife must be very sharp and must have a slight burr on the underneath side. Directions for sharpening knives were given in Chapter XIII, p. 76. When the leather has been evenly pared the outlined tools desired for inlaying should be impressed, while cold, on the leather, which is cut to the shape with a sharp, pointed knife or scissors. The small circles used in Fig. 88, p. 97, are more easily cut out with a punch of the required size. Steel punches may also be made to fit any of the other tools if much inlaying is to be done.

When the inlays have been cut out in the various colours they should be laid, colour side up, on a piece of glass or the paring stone which has been pasted with fairly thick paste. They should be rubbed down on to the paste with a sheet of paper so that they will be pasted evenly, the paper removed, and each inlay picked up with the point of a fine folder and placed in position over the blinded impression. Rubbing them down through a sheet of paper will make them stick well in the impressions, and in doing this care must be taken not to move them out of their places. When the inlays are dry the tools, warmed slightly only, should be worked in again over them. When preparing the leather for gold tooling after inlaying, care should be taken in washing with vinegar or paste water that the inlays are not removed. When the preparation dries, the impressions should be glaired-in and tooled as described before.

CHAPTER XVI

PASTING DOWN OPEN AND
FINISHING OUT

When a flexible sewn book, half- or full-bound leather, has been 'finished', the next process is to paste down the end-papers.

Before pasting down, both boards of the book should be opened, and the book placed over a pressing board just up to the joint, as in Fig. 96.

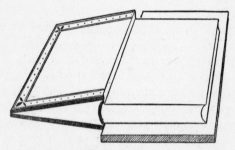

Fig. 96. Method of pasting down open

The waste sheets are then torn off and the joint cleared of glue or paste with the point of a knife. Care must be taken not to cut the leather which comes between the board and the book. The paste-down end-paper should be lifted, stretched over the board and rubbed down squarely over the joint. With a pair of dividers set to the inside line of the leather margin the three edges should be marked by pricking two points on each side, measuring from the edge of the board. A cutting-tin should be placed on the book, the paste-down sheets laid over this, and cuts made from point to point with a sharp-pointed knife and straight-edge. So that small pieces may be left at the head and tail of the end-paper to cover the edge of the board in the joint, the paper should only

be cut to the crease made when bringing the paper over the top
of the joint (*Fig. 97*).

When both paste-down papers are cut to the required size, a
piece of waste paper should be placed underneath to protect the
book, and the end-papers should be pasted well with medium
thick paste, especially in the joint. After pasting, the finger should
be rubbed down the joint to make sure that it has been well and
evenly pasted. All lumps should be removed and the pasted paper

Fig. 97. Method of cutting out end-papers

brought over on to the board, adjusted exactly in position, and
rubbed down with the hand. A piece of clean paper should be
laid over and the end-paper rubbed well down in the joint through
the waste sheet, which prevents the surface becoming either shiny
or roughened.

It is important that the paper should stick well to all three parts
of the joint, the book, the leather or hinge, and the edge of the
board.

When one side has been pasted down, the book must be turned
over without shutting the board and the other end-paper pasted
down in the same way. The joints should be examined and rubbed
down again, as some end-papers are apt to lift unless properly
soaked with paste. The boards of
the book must be left open on the
pressing board (*Fig. 96*), with the
boards held back by a piece of
cardboard cut as Fig. 98, until the
end-papers are dry.

*Fig. 98. End section of Fig. 96
showing method of holding
boards open till dry*

When the end-papers are dry—and the time for this varies with different papers—the book must be carefully closed. Care must be taken that the paper folds just at the joint between the board and the book. Tins lined with paper should be placed inside each board and a sheet or two of paper on the outside of each cover. The whole should then be placed between smooth pressing boards, put into the press and left there for a few hours (*Fig. 56. p. 56*).

POLISHING. When the book is taken out of the press it should be examined to see that all the processes previously described have been executed correctly. Polishing is the next process, if that is required for the book.

If the book has been covered in such leathers as morocco, or seal, the grain is usually crushed before finishing, and it is only necessary now to give a final polish. The usual polisher is as Fig. 24, p. 15; has a polishing surface of smooth steel. Polishers must be used warm, but not too hot. Before using they must be cleaned very carefully on a knife-board or with bath-brick rubbed on to a piece of straw- or millboard. The back of the book is usually polished first, moving the polisher up and down between each band. When all the panels are polished in one direction, the book should be turned round and polished again so that the edge of the polisher may be used right up to each side of the bands in each panel.

The back cover is then polished by using the polisher from tail to head, taking great care to press in the middle of the polisher, or the outside edges will mark the leather. The book is then turned round and the polisher used from head to tail, turned again and polished from back to fore-edge and the reverse. A beautiful polish or lustre on the leather should result. The front cover is then treated in the same manner, and a lasting polished surface will be secured if a light coat of 'Bookbinder's French Varnish' is applied. This is done with a pad of cotton wool dipped in varnish, rubbed on paper to distribute it, and put on the book quickly with a circular motion. If too much varnish is applied it will tarnish the gold and spoil its brilliancy, but the advantage of varnishing is that the book may then be handled without the fear of finger marks showing.

CHAPTER XVII

TWO METHODS OF MARBLING

There are two methods of marbling now in general use, one using Carragheen Moss size together with specially prepared colours, and the other with oil colours and ordinary size. The former allows more scope for variety, but the latter may be found more convenient for elementary school purposes. Both methods are therefore given.

Little is actually known about the origin of marbling, a discovery which has made possible a great variety of beautiful combinations of colour on paper for decorative purposes. Various theories have been advanced. Some claim it to be of Dutch origin, others of French or German; but modern research tends to show that marbling was an Eastern conceit; that is to say, the idea of throwing colours on water alone, or water strengthened with size, and lifting the colours on sheets of paper, was first conceived and practised in the East.

The earliest mention of the process, so far as the writer is aware, was made by Lord Bacon in *Sylva Sylvarum* (1627). 'The Turks', says he, 'have a pretty art of chamoletting of paper, which is not with us in use. They take divers oyled colours and put them severally (in drops) upon water; and stirre the water lightly, and then wet thin paper with it, and the paper will be waved, and veined, like chamolet or marble.' An album in the Art Library at South Kensington containing examples of marbled papers, collected by one Wolffgang Leutkauff, of Vienna, who left Vienna in 1616 for Constantinople, from which city he journeyed through Adrianople and Philippopoli, appears to bear out the contention that marbling was of Eastern origin. These papers were first used for decorative purposes, such as the groundwork of manuscripts, or backing of illuminations; later they were more particularly used for end-papers and covers of books.

With the increasing recognition of colour work in the various crafts now practised in schools, marbling will be found to be an ideal subject for teaching colour sense. It is one of the simplest methods of expression in colour; by its use pleasing effects can be produced which are unobtainable by any other means. It would be as well, however, before demonstrating this process, that the teacher should give some simple instruction in the principles of colour harmony, and contrast and discord should be explained and demonstrated by reference to the solar spectrum, or 'colour circle'.

Since its introduction various methods of marbling have been employed. The earliest, and possibly the most simple, was that of throwing oil colours on size, but this method has its limitations. Later, vegetable colours were ground with beeswax, curd soap, and water, and thrown on a size made from gum tragacanth, but this is a lengthy and troublesome process, and quite unsuitable for schools.

A simpler method is now in use. Specially prepared colours may be had ready for working on a size made from Carragheen moss (Irish seaweed). This process was discovered by Josef Halfer, of Budapest, and found wide acceptance in Germany, Austria and Hungary. This is the process that will be here described.

METHOD I. WITH CARRAGHEEN MOSS SIZE AND PREPARED COLOURS

Utensils and Apparatus Required

A *Trough* to hold the size upon which the colours are thrown. This should be made of tin, a convenient size being 22 in. by

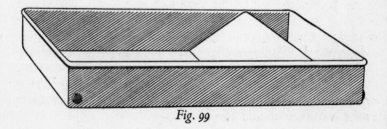

Fig. 99

11 in. and 1½ in. deep. The interior space of the trough must be divided by a sloping partition 3 in. from the right-hand end; the smaller division serves to hold the waste colour (*see Fig. 99*). The interior of the trough should be coated with white enamel, in order that the operator may observe the colours and judge their intensity. The exterior may be painted any colour to preserve it from rust.

Enamelled Cups. These are for holding the colours. Six will be required.

Combs. For comb patterns four combs with variously spaced teeth are necessary. The most useful are four teeth to the inch, and two teeth to the inch. Also a double comb in which the spacing is wide and narrow alternately: say ½ in. and ¼ in. teeth alternately.

These combs may be made by the students, as follows: Cut two strips of millboard or strawboard about ⅛ in. thick, 10½ in. long and 2 in. wide. Measure off, with the dividers, the required division of the teeth, and cut these divisions 1 in. from lower edge of the board, and sufficiently deep so that 2 in. needles may lie firmly embedded in them, and flush with the surface. Glue the strip and place the needles 1 in. within the slots, leaving the

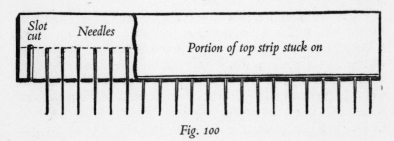

Fig. 100

pointed end of the needles projecting 1 in. beyond the lower edge or strip. Glue the second strip on to the first, with needles between and either put in press or under a heavy weight to dry (*Fig. 100*).

Brushes. The most suitable brushes for marbling are made of hog bristles, and are about ½ in. in diameter with at least 1½ in.

length of bristles, which should be mounted in tin. The bristles must be curved (*Fig. 101*).

Rice-straw Brushes. For sprinkling the colours in small spots a rice-straw brush will be needed. These are made from soft rice straw and are from ¾ in. to 1½ in. wide. The bristles are bound to the handle with copper wire (*Fig. 102*).

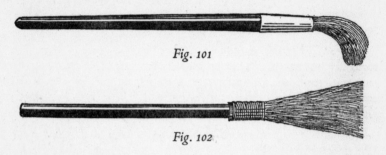

Fig. 101

Fig. 102

A Stylus Point. This is for raking the colours. A fine gimlet or bodkin will meet the case.

The Size

The size or ground on which the colours are floated is made from Carragheen moss (Irish seaweed).

Take 1 oz. moss and two quarts rain water. The water should be put into a four-quart saucepan and put on the fire, when boiling the 1 oz. moss should be put in and boiled for five minutes, stirring all the while so that it does not boil over. As soon as the moss and water have boiled the requisite time, take the saucepan from the fire and add one pint of cold water, stirring the size meanwhile. While the size is hot it should not be covered. It should be kept in a cool place or it will turn brackish. After allowing it to stand twenty-four hours strain it through a linen bag into the trough. Care should be taken not to squeeze the bag too much or the size will not be clear.

Ox Gall. This is better bought ready prepared for use. Fresh gall is unsuitable, as the water-colours which are used in marbling will not mix with the fatty parts of the gall.

Veining Liquid is needed for certain kinds of marbling, and is made as follows: To 2 oz. spirit of soap add 1⅛ pints of rain water, shake it well, and the veining liquid is ready for use.

Alum Water is prepared as follows: To 1 oz. crystallized alum add 1 pint rain water and boil till the alum is dissolved, pour into bottles, and keep well corked.

The alum has the property of absorbing the colours, and renders them more adhesive. The edges of the book or paper to be marbled should be sponged over with the alum water, and the marbling should be done while it is still damp, but not wet.

Preparation and Mixing of Colours

The colours as supplied all need mixing with either gall or veining liquid, according to the kind of marbling to be done and the effect desired.

For combed patterns the colours must be prepared as follows:

First shake the bottle well to bring up the sediment, pour two-thirds of an ounce of each colour—say blue, green, yellow, and red—into separate pots, and add to each six drops of prepared ox gall; place a brush in each and stir well.

For 'Turkish', i.e. veined and spot patterns, the colours should be prepared according to the following instructions: 1st black; to ¾ oz. of colour add 6 drops of gall. 2nd blue or red; ½ oz. of colour 1 oz. soft water and 12 drops of gall. 3rd gall water; 1½ oz. of water and 12 drops of prepared ox gall. 4th or ground colour; 1 oz. of brown (or any other colour desired) and ½ oz. of veining liquid.

Method of Marbling

Marbling is best done over or near a sink, because running water is needed for washing off the size and superfluous colour after the paper has been dipped.

Before commencing to marble it will be necessary to see that everything is ready to hand, because speed is an important factor to success. The sheets of paper to be marbled must be cut to size and sponged over with alum water. Plenty of newspaper strips must be cut 12 in. by 3 in. for skimming the surface of the size. The size must be strained into the trough, all colours prepared, and combs and stylus to hand.

I

Method of Throwing on Colours for Combed and Raked Patterns (see sample 3, on Plate IX, which shows the effect of raking with a stylus only).

1. Before throwing the colours on, skim the surface of the size with a strip of newspaper, in order to remove any skin which will have formed.

2. Stir up each colour with its brush and place at the back of the trough in the following order: blue, green, yellow, red.

3. Blue is the first colour to be used; after blue comes green, which is dropped on the blue in two rows of drops. After green comes yellow, which should be dropped on the green. The fourth colour, red, is dropped on the yellow.

4. The first colour used must spread at least five inches in diameter.

5. The size must be reduced with water until this result is attained. After adding the water stir well with the hand, so that the size is of even consistency. Skim off the surface of the size again with newspaper, and try colour again; if it spreads to the required dimensions the size will be right; if not, more water must be added.

This skimming of the size immediately before the colours are dropped on is of the utmost importance, as if a film is allowed to form the colours will not spread at all.

6. Now drop spots of blue, which should cover the surface of the size, then green, then yellow, lastly red.

7. When all the colours are dropped on the size, draw serpentine lines with the stylus point from front to back of the trough.

8. Then draw the comb evenly across from left to right, the teeth just touching the surface of the size. The motion should be faster with a wide than a narrow comb.

9. Take hold of the sheet of paper (with the alumed side downwards) by the bottom left-hand corner with the left hand, and the top right-hand corner with the right hand, and proceed to lay it upon the surface of the size. Start at the botton left-hand corner, and gradually lower the paper towards the right-hand

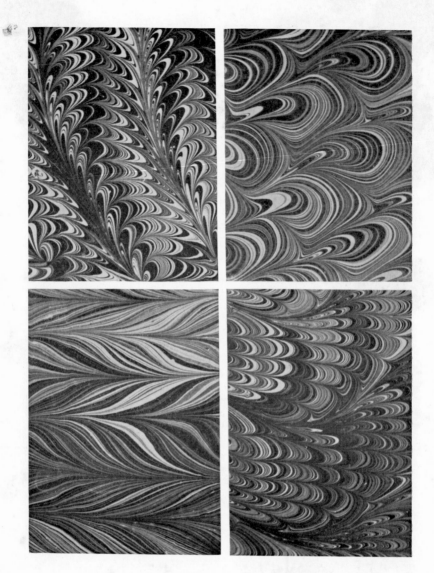

PLATE IX
Marbling: four examples of combed or raked patterns.

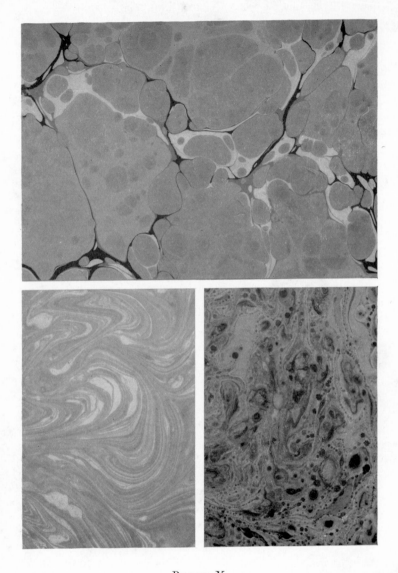

PLATE X

Above: A 'Turkish' or 'Stone Marble' pattern.
Below: Two examples of Oil Marbling.

corner, until the paper lies perfectly flat upon the surface of the size. Lift up the paper, and wash off the surplus colour and size with water, under a gently running tap, hang up or lay out to dry.

If it is the edges of a book that are to be marbled, place the book between two boards, knock level to the edge, grip tightly in both hands, and lower it on to the size, commencing at one corner and gradually bring the other corner down. The surplus colour is then washed off, being careful not to let the water run in the edges, and the book left to dry.

Method of Throwing on Colour for 'Turkish' or 'Stone Marble'.

1. The colours are prepared according to instructions on page 113 and the size must be rather thinner than for comb patterns.

2. The first colour must expand about seven inches, and the size must be reduced with water until the desired expansion is attained.

3. The second colour must be sprinkled with a rice-straw brush on the first colour in very small drops.

4. The gall water for producing white veins in the marble must be sprinkled on the first and second colours in a similar way.

5. The ground colour has to be sprinkled in large drops over first, second, and third colour.

6. Dip paper and wash off as before described.

General Observations

Always shake the bottles well before pouring out the colours.

Prepare the paper or book edges with alum water and let them dry for about ten minutes before marbling.

Marbling colours are soft, and therefore must be used on a soft size.

Pay particular attention to the preparation of the size. Success or failure very largely depends upon this.

Do not keep the size longer than six days; after this period it turns sour and is useless.

The colours, after being thrown on to the size in spots, may be raked, combed, or swirled in a great variety of ways, producing many different patterns.

Dry comb and stylus each time, after using, with a duster.

Many interesting patterns can be marbled by the use of two colours only, the tint of the paper forming another or ground colour.

The particular value of this method of marbling, as a school subject, is that it gives great scope for individual treatment or 'free expression'.

METHOD II. WITH ORDINARY SIZE AND OIL COLOURS

Oil Colour Marbling

This method of marbling was suggested to the writer when reading Lord Bacon's *Sylva Sylvarum* (1627), as quoted at the beginning of this chapter.

After considerable experiment, the following method was evolved, which will be found quite simple and effective. Although such definite patterns cannot be obtained by this method as by the orthodox Trade marbling, it can be more easily taught in elementary schools, as the apparatus and materials required are not so costly, and the size and colours can be mixed by the students themselves.

Apparatus and Materials required

A Tin Trough (as illustrated on p. 110) to hold the size. A baking tin, with sloping sides, would serve very well, a useful size being 18 in. by 12 in.

Several Small Jars, for holding the mixed colours; these should be deep enough to hold the brushes upright.

Brushes, for mixing the oil colours and throwing them on to the size. The one specially made, with curved bristles, is best for this purpose, but any large water-colour brush will do.

Combs. These may be made by the students, as described and illustrated on page 111.

Stylus. For raking the colours; a gimlet or pencil will do.

Paper. Any soft sized papers are suitable—e.g. printings, cartridge, tinted pastels, thin light-coloured wrapping papers—cream, buff, and green.

Size. Ordinary powdered size in 1 lb. packets is best, but good cake glue will serve.

Oil Colours. Oil colours or printing inks in tubes.

Paraffin Oil. For thinning the oil colours.

Turpentine. For thinning printing inks.

NOTE. Either thinner may be used, but not both at the same time.

Newspaper. Cut half the size of the trough—for clearing the size.

To Make the Size. Dissolve 2 oz. of size or 2 oz. of good hot glue in one pint of boiling water, stir until the size or glue is completely dissolved. Pour into the trough and add about five pints of cold water. The size is better made a day before it is required for use. When cold it should not appear gelatinous but quite liquid.

To Prepare the Oil Colours. Squeeze about 2 in. of each colour required into separate jars, and add about a teaspoonful of paraffin. Stir until the colour is dissolved.

Ivory black, red or orange, blue, green, will be found to give a great variety of colour schemes.

Cut the paper required for marbling a shade smaller than the size of the trough.

Newspaper half the size.

Having prepared the size and mixed the colours (not more than three), place the trough on a table or bench and the jars of colour each with its own brush at the back of the trough, and see that everything required is ready to hand.

To Test the Colours. First draw a piece of newspaper over the surface of the size to remove any film which may have formed. This is best done by placing the paper up to the left-hand side of the trough, letting it rest on the size, and draw across to the right. Now drop spots of colour on to the size. If the colour sinks, or remains on the surface in very small spots, it is too thick, and should be thinned with a little more paraffin. If the colour spreads too much and seems to vanish, it is too thin, and a little more colour must be added.

A few experiments will be necessary before satisfactory results can be obtained, and tests should be made on small pieces of paper.

Method of Working. First clear the size with newspaper, then throw spots of colour all over the surface of the size and work up the pattern by slowly drawing the stylus through the colours; either from back to front or in a circular or wavy direction. When a pleasing result has been obtained, take a piece of paper to be marbled by opposite edges and gently lower it on to the surface of the size, being careful to see that the whole sheet is in contact with the size. Lift by again taking hold of opposite edges and allow the superfluous size to drain into the trough. Hang up or place on sheets of newspaper to dry.

By again raking the colour left on the size, a second pattern may be taken off, sometimes more pleasing than the first, as the colours will be fainter, giving a softer effect.

General Observations

The size should be from $\frac{3}{4}$ in. to 1 in. deep in the trough, and will last about a fortnight.

If comb patterns are desired, first rake the colours, with the stylus, from back to front and then draw the comb slowly through from left to right.

One colour only will make very pleasing patterns and will be found very suitable for end-papers.

When dry the marbled sheet may be burnished by passing a warm iron over the surface.

Purposes for which the marbled paper may be used:
Covering of small notebooks and pamphlets.
End-papers for leather bound books.
Sides for half- and quarter- bound books.
Covering of cardboard boxes and calendars.

CHAPTER XVIII

THE GRAINING AND STAINING OF PAPER FOR END-PAPERS AND COVERS

The student will find not only an attraction but a definite practical advantage in making his own end-papers or cover papers. They may be designed to harmonize with the linen or leather used and made to add a very personal touch to the binding.

Paper. The papers used may be white, cream or tinted; they should be of fairly good quality and not too thin. The surface may be matt or smooth, according to the nature of the decorative effect desired. Cartridge papers give good results, but if a polished surface is required a smooth paper must be used.

Brushes. Several fairly stiff, flat brushes, from 1 in. to 2 in. wide, are needed to apply the colour (*Fig. 103*).

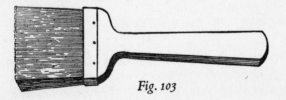

Fig. 103

Combs. Various metal graining combs may be obtained from painters and decorators. Some of the teeth of these should be cut out at regular or irregular intervals to give a variety of patterns (*Fig. 104*). Combs may also be cut by the student from thin celluloid.

Stamps. Pieces of wood of different widths cut to chisel points are useful for making patterns of single or broken lines, and stamps may be cut from linoleum and fixed on corks (*Fig. 105*).

With this apparatus there need be no limit to the variety and interest of pattern, and if the student is allowed latitude and fun in the application of colour and the method of working, surprising and ingenious results will be obtained.

Colour. Tempera colours in powder are convenient to use, and students' water-colours in tubes give smooth and clear results.

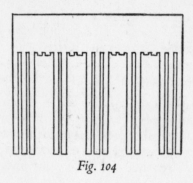

Fig. 104

Fig. 105

Pastes. The paste required may be made with starch. In making this a tablespoonful of powdered starch should be placed in a basin with enough cold water to make it the consistency of thick cream and stirred till it is absolutely free from lumps. Quite boiling water should be added until the mixture becomes clear.

Gloy sold in bottles also makes a good and clean medium for mixing with the colours; is always ready for use, and keeps fresh indefinitely.

If powdered colour is used a quantity should be placed in a saucer and just sufficient water added to dissolve the powder. Starch paste or Gloy should be mixed with this to give the consistency of cream. The colour should not be so thick that it will

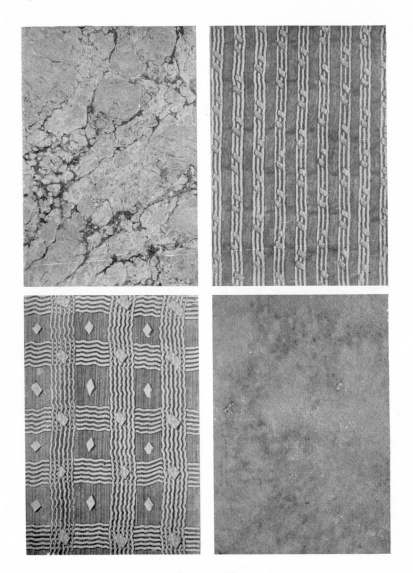

PLATE XI

Four examples of Grained and Stained Papers.

dry in ridges when combed, but it must be thick enough to stand up against the comb.

Tube colours are mixed in the same way, and enough colour must be mixed to cover completely whatever size sheet of paper is to be used.

Experiments should be made on small pieces of paper first. Then, if end-papers are required, the paper used must be large enough to make both at once. If possible, this should not be larger than demy (22½ in. by 17½ in.) or the colour will dry before the pattern can be completed.

Applying Colour. The sheet to be grained should be placed on a drawing board and damped evenly all over with a sponge. Colour should be applied with a large brush to cover the whole surface, and should be evenly distributed by working the brush in straight lines from head to tail or from left to right. A broken surface is obtained by dabbing or stippling with the brush.

Patterns may be made entirely by the brush, using it the thin way to make a series of lines, down the coloured surface, or dabbing it on the plain background.

If the student wishes to grain the paper with a comb or stamp he must proceed quickly while the colour is still wet, and should a tinted background be used the colour will be revealed when the body colour is scraped away with the comb.

The illustrations give an indication of the variety of pattern to be obtained.

A burnished surface may be made by rubbing over the paper with a warm flat-iron or a bookbinder's polisher (*Fig. 24*), and the sheets may be made damp-proof by adding a little water-glass when mixing the colour.

Staining or Colouring. A similar type of paper may be used for staining or colouring as for graining. Moist water-colours or dyes in powder or coloured inks may be applied.

The paper is first well damped with a sponge, or even held under the tap, and the colours then thrown on with large camel-hair brushes and blended by letting them run, one into another. When the dyes or inks have struck into the paper they should be washed off under the tap, and hung up to dry. Water-colours should not be washed off, but the paper should be left flat to dry. In running colours together, blotting paper may be used to prevent further combination when the desired effect has been obtained.

The surface may be ironed or polished, as in the case of grained papers.

These processes may be made interesting exercises in colour mixing and blending, and as such are useful not only to the child but to the older student as an aid to the appreciation of colour. In the early teaching of the properties of colour the exercise in staining might be limited to the use of the three primaries, and practical experience given, in a fascinating manner, of their possibilities and limitations.

INDEX